"Though this book is made ... Lesson is intentionally crafted ... ...ights for people in all stages of life. These Life Lessons are personal, raw, and genuinely inspiring."

—**Brandon Luarca**, marketing specialist

"I wish I could time travel just so I could take this book back to my past self. The simplest of advice goes a long way when you're new to the real world. Incredible advice from such amazing souls. Thank you all for sharing!"

—**Sarai Mendoza**, bilingual aide

"This book has been so helpful for me! It offers priceless advice on how to learn from your social, personal, and academic struggles to find your true purpose in life."

—**Danica Gressel**, graduate student in chemistry

"Life is tricky to figure out. Reading other people's advice is a valuable tool to have. It is especially valuable for this book to have examples of how to put this advice into action. All recent graduates can benefit from reading this book."

—**Emily Ryschon**, college student

"This book has a wide variety of wonderful advice for those who are ready to embark on their next step after graduation. Many of the topics provide relatable real-life examples and great tips for navigating through day-to-day experiences."

—**Courtney Knapp**, human services
case management supervisor

"The contributors to this book provide practical advice for recent graduates and young professionals. The chapter on engaging with introverted people was very informative as it helped me apply the principle to my personal and professional life!"

—**Fergus Cheung**, U.S. Army officer

"This book does not fake it and can prepare anyone awaiting or undergoing change. It does an excellent job addressing the struggle of transition and offers advice for those who are about to experience life's growing pains."

—**Abby Campbell**, college student

"*50 Life Lessons for Grads* is such a thoughtful book that truly captures lessons that many of us overlook as we make the transition from graduation to adult life, lessons that are so relevant to our everyday success and self-fulfillment. It was such a breath of fresh air to read about other people's *aha!* moments and relating those moments to my own similar experiences post-graduation. This book was a joy to read and will have true meaning and value to students starting their journey after graduation."

—**Haley Seeger**, assistant operations manager for a ranch

"This book is full of truths and advice that would be beneficial to any graduate who can embrace the fact that there is still so much to learn about life."

—**Danielle Shotwell**, physical therapist

"*50 Life Lessons for Grads* is a great read for any young person just getting a start in life. It's challenging and grounding, and it would make a great gift!"

—**Sarah Walsh**, registered nurse

"Whether it's a lesson in moving on or moving out or simply a moving story, this book has something to offer everyone, be they grads or returning students."

—Rachel Huebert-Wheeler, stablehand

"This book was uniquely different from anything I have ever read. With stories from real graduates plus related Scriptures, this book is highly recommended."

—Nicole Miller, recent graduate

"Insightful, authentic, and overflowing with wisdom, *50 Life Lessons for Grads* provides powerful testimony, demonstrating that experiencing and overcoming many of life's challenges makes us more resilient and wiser in our future."

—Angelo Genasci, entrepreneur

"*50 Life Lessons for Grads* is not only inspirational for graduates, but can also be refreshing for everyone. These heartfelt lessons teach you the importance of life and will have you encouraged to keep on going."

—Samantha Walker, new mom

"This is an absolutely genius read! From a good laugh to a time of reflection, the reading of advice on such a variety of topics is so helpful."

—Anna Magaña Manzano, teacher

"*50 Life Lessons for Grads* provides insightful advice from recent graduates about following God's path. All graduates will be encouraged by the writer's steadfast faith."

—Lauren Hennessey, physician assistant student

"Such an uplifting and motivating book. I loved how thought provoking and applicable each story was to my own life. It is a super easy read and something every graduate should add to their book collection."

—**Kaelen Mora**, two boys' mama

"A wonderful, faith-based must-read for all graduates who are entering a workforce where simply having a college degree no longer gives you an edge."

—**Kasey DeAtley**, university professor
in animal and range science

50
LIFE LESSONS
for
GRADS

50
LIFE LESSONS
for
GRADS

Surprising Advice
from Recent Graduates

GENERAL EDITOR
JANET HOLM MCHENRY

WORTHY®
Inspired

50 Life Lessons for Grads
© Copyright 2018 Janet Holm McHenry

Published by Worthy Inspired, an imprint of Worthy Publishing Group, a division of Worthy Media, Inc., One Franklin Park, 6100 Tower Circle, Suite 210, Franklin, TN 37067.

WORTHY is a registered trademark of Worthy Media, Inc.

HELPING PEOPLE EXPERIENCE THE HEART OF GOD.

eBook available wherever digital books are sold.

Library of Congress Control Number: 2017960761

Published in association with the Books & Such Literary Management, 52 Mission Circle, Suite 122, PMB 170, Santa Rosa, CA 95409-5370, www.booksandsuch.com.

ISBN 978-1-68397-046-0

Cover design by Jeff Jansen | AestheticSoup.com
Cover art by Shutterstock
Interior design by Bart Dawson

Printed in the United States of America

1 2 3 4 5 6 7 8 9 LBM 23 22 21 20 19 18

CONTENTS

**Listen to advice
and accept discipline,
and at the end you will be
counted among the wise.**

Proverbs 19:20

Introduction

Congratulations! You've done it, graduate! It's cap-throwing time! You have finished your exams. You have thanked your hard-working educators. (You did thank them, right?) And you have proven you have mastered those crazy academics and are ready for the adult world.

It will be hard saying good-bye to friends who have been walking the same path you have for the last handful of years, but there are exciting opportunities ahead for you. Now you get to put what you have learned into place—whether that involves more education or the workplace or the military.

In any case, what you will soon find out is that there is still a lot to learn, the most important of which may be what we are calling Life Lessons—those intangible fuzzies that you do not learn in an English or history classroom. Instead, they will come in *aha!* moments, such as when you get sick for the very first time without your mom around.

So you call her. "Mom, I am so sick. I really need your advice about what to do."

And Mom is probably silent for a minute. She may, in fact, be in shock. Finally she says, "Could you please repeat that? I thought you said you needed my advice."

After she has told you to take a pain reliever and drink lots of fluids and go to bed, there it is—that *aha!* moment.

Ohmygoodness! My mom is a genius. Why didn't I notice it before?

Some of those lessons you will probably have to learn on your own. However, others have gone before you and have had their share of *aha!* moments that have gelled into Life Lessons. And they would like to share them with you so you don't have to learn everything the hard way. Read, enjoy . . . and keep learning.

Friendships are worth pursuing.

Annie Maddalena Tipton

I cannot count how many times in my life I missed an opportunity to make a simple gesture of kindness. When a friend was suffering from a loss or feeling down, I would think I should call him/her or send a card. But typically, I would get caught up in the activities of my busy life, and time would pass by, resulting in a missed opportunity. I would justify it by telling myself that it didn't really matter if she or he heard from me—I couldn't make a difference.

Eventually, I lost touch with some of those friends but later realized that there was a void in my life—I really missed them! So I made a conscious decision to change this. I started sending not only birthday cards but also encouragement, get well, sympathy, and thinking-of-you

3

cards. I also picked up the phone and called friends and family.

After a few short weeks, I couldn't believe the difference. Just through small acts of kindness and effort, my relationships with those around me became much more meaningful. Because I took time to reestablish or increase my contact with these people, they realized that I truly valued our friendship. To this day, I jump on the opportunity to let a friend know she or he is in my thoughts and prayers, because to someone feeling disheartened or alone, this could make a real difference.

Annie Tipton has degrees in agricultural business and liberal studies from California State University, Chico. She is an elementary school teacher.

GOD'S LIFE LESSON

Do not forsake your friend.

PROVERBS 27:10

LIVING THE LESSON

- Write thank-you notes for your graduation gifts and add a special note about how that person has helped or encouraged you.

- Write thank-you notes to educators and others who have guided you in recent years.

- Several times a year, send a handwritten note to someone just to tell that person why he or she is special to you.

- Do more than say "Happy birthday!" on Facebook to those closest to you. Send a real card through snail mail.

- When you hear that something good has happened in someone's life, send a simple note of congratulations. It will mean a lot.

- Send sympathy cards to those going through loss—they will read them over and over as they need strength for the days ahead.

Money isn't everything.

Ryan Knapp

Around the time I graduated college, I was working as a meteorologist at a flight tower in San Jose, a job that paid me handsomely but wasn't fulfilling. My coworkers were great, but the desk job wasn't what I had pictured—it was much more reminiscent of the characters in *Twister* than those from *The Office*. While I was updating my resume, I stumbled upon a website for the Mount Washington Observatory, a remote summit station that has some of the lowest temperatures and highest wind ever recorded. An unpaid internship was available for a few months—with no certainty of a paid position. After much thought and prayer, I made the leap and transported myself three thousand miles away from my comfort zone in California to New Hampshire.

While life was challenging during that unpaid internship, a full-time meteorologist position soon opened up. Even still, the income would be only half of what I had been earning at the airport. Practically speaking, it seemed to be a huge leap backward for my career, but God made it clear that He would provide for all my needs. Now I am working my dream job—doing research for a private, non-profit, scientific and educational institution whose mission is to advance understanding of the natural systems that create the earth's weather and climate. It's one of those jobs that makes you want to go to work, that makes you happy inside and out. Even today, while I might be making less than half of what I used to make, I'm doing something that is twice as enjoyable.

Ryan Knapp has a BS in meteorology from California State University, San Jose. He is a meteorologist, researcher, and weather observer.

GOD'S LIFE LESSON

And my God will meet
all your needs according to the riches
of his glory in Christ Jesus.

PHILIPPIANS 4:19

LIVING THE LESSON

- Take one week this summer to job shadow several different occupations that interest you to see what the work is really like.

- Focus more on being a giver rather than a taker at your job. You'll find that your work takes on more meaning as you dial in to what others need instead of focusing on your own takeaway.

- Even if a job isn't particularly rewarding, do your best; it could lead to a new position that would better suit you.

- Study the mission of the company. If you believe in an organization's mission, you will find your work makes a difference, even if your daily tasks aren't so exciting.

- Volunteer for a local charity. People who are less fortunate will appreciate your help, and perhaps you will find an important life purpose.

Waiting can bring unexpected blessings.

Sarah Cheek Buckner

I have learned many important lessons since graduating high school, but the most important is that the happily-ever-after movie ending doesn't always happen as you think it should. Life does not always turn out as planned, so it's important to remain flexible to God's direction. Wonderful life experiences can happen while you're waiting for the right job or right marriage partner.

When I was in high school, my life plan involved going to college and then finding my happily-ever-after, which was getting married and having a family. Period. My actual path started out in that direction, because I did obtain my college degree, but I waited more than ten years for the happily-ever-after part.

I didn't sit idle for those ten years after college graduation, though. To help process my singleness, I started what became a popular blog that quickly amassed thousands of followers, some of whom became friends who encouraged me. My career changed during this time, too. I began with a rewarding job teaching high school history students. Eventually, I returned to college to do graduate work, and now I counsel high school students with their academic goals.

I know that the ten years I waited to meet my future husband were crucial so that I would get to know him at the right point in *his* life. While I will probably always be a planner and a scheduler, I have learned to be open to God's timing.

Like me, you might find that God's plans don't completely align with yours. While you wait, I encourage you to find ways to live your life in a positive and productive manner.

———————————————————————

Sarah Buckner has a degree in sociology from Appalachian State University and another in education from Texas Christian University, as well as a master's degree in counseling from Lamar University. She works as a high school counselor.

GOD'S LIFE LESSON

—————————

"For I know the plans I have for you,"
declares the LORD, "plans to prosper
you and not to harm you,
plans to give you hope and a future."

JEREMIAH 29:11

LIVING THE LESSON

- Make a list of the qualities you want in a future spouse.

- Pray regularly for God's direction for your life.

- If you're in a relationship wait mode, take up a hobby that you've always wanted to pursue, such as ceramics or guitar lessons.

- Waiting can produce stress, and that can tax your body. Make healthy diet choices and exercise several times a week.

- If you're waiting on a job prospect, stay current in the literature of your field. Read well-researched articles and books, so that a future employer can see your dedication to your career.

Love is a choice.

Shelia Provoast Hail

Much of what we learn about love as we grow is contradictory. Some say that love never fails. Others say they fell out of love. What I have learned is that, while love *is* something I feel, it is also a choice. So, if someone says she has fallen out of love, the truth is simply that she chose not to love anymore.

This lesson became real to me when I met my husband, Matt. From the beginning of our relationship when I was a junior in college, we were apart—he in Nashville and I in Oregon. So many uncertainties and even fear built up within me, and not seeing him made matters more difficult. I soon realized I had to learn to trust and choose to love him. I also had to choose to believe and trust that he loved me.

Now that we are married, I understand the truth of that statement even more. I have learned that love is not just "in the air." Every morning, Matt and I wake up to a new day, and we must choose to love and trust each other. Some days are easier than others to feel love, to trust without concern. But when the feelings aren't there, we can still choose to love, to trust, and to receive love from each other. Truthfully, if we relied solely on feelings, we would have "fallen out of love" long ago. By the grace of God, love has been the best choice we've ever made.

Shelia Hail has a degree in communications from George Fox University. She writes for an online magazine, manages a home decor website, works at a clothing boutique, and runs her and her husband's cinematography business.

GOD'S LIFE LESSON

Love never fails.

1 CORINTHIANS 13:8

LIVING THE LESSON

- Notice the love choices that married couples make. Thank them for being good examples to you.

- Demonstrate love in a tangible way today—even just a sticky note left in the right place.

- Actively listen and engage in conversation with that someone you say you love. Put your cell phone away, look at the other person, and respond in a positive, caring manner without critical or judgmental comments.

- Defer to the other person's choice of a restaurant or movie selection.

- Notice the good work that someone does and compliment him or her for a job well done.

Each person has value.

Josh Davis

Einstein was quoted as saying, "Everybody is a genius. But if you judge a fish by its ability to climb a tree, it will live its whole life believing that it is stupid." Not only do all people have intrinsic value, they have specific value. I'm smart. I learn quickly. I have many God-given talents. But there are some things I don't do well.

I learned to appreciate others and their abilities through two coworkers, Steve and Joe. Steve was so critical of almost everyone that some made friends with him to avoid being his target. Joe was a mechanic. Steve was always quick to remind Joe where he stood on the ladder, but Joe took it in stride. He'd always smile and say something like, "You're good at what you do; I'm good at what I do." He never bit back or offered Steve the least bit of sourness.

One day, as we were leaving work, Steve's car wouldn't start. Instead of calling Joe and asking him to take a look at it, he took it apart himself, right there in the parking lot. One hour and a completely disassembled alternator later, Steve finally called Joe, who showed up within minutes. He put the alternator back together, reinstalled it, found and fixed the actual problem, shook Steve's hand, and smiled. "Thanks for asking me to help you, Steve," he said. "I enjoy helping my friends." Though the look on Steve's face was priceless, the thing I remember most was seeing the satisfaction in Joe's eyes—not that he had finally pulled one over on Steve, but rather that he was legitimately able to help one of his friends. From then on, Steve did not make fun of Joe's occupation.

This taught me that everyone has value in this world, so we shouldn't make fools of ourselves trying to put others in "their place."

Josh Davis studied pastoral counseling and youth ministry at Grand Canyon University and currently works as a full-time youth pastor at his church.

GOD'S LIFE LESSON

Whoever wants to become great
among you must be your servant,
and whoever wants to be first
must be slave of all.

MARK 10:43–44

LIVING THE LESSON

- Make it a point this week to thank three people who physically work hard for their living.

- Help your family out at home today by doing something without being asked first.

- Take interest in your hair stylist by asking him or her sincere questions about his or her background and work.

- If you see a homeless person by a fast-food spot, buy him a burger and have a short conversation with him.

- Demonstrate respect for wait staff at restaurants by cleaning up your mess at the table and leaving a decent tip.

A lot of a little equals a lot.

Amanda Church Osburn

Have you ever gotten on the scale and, having gained five pounds, thought, "I really haven't eaten that much this week. Well, there was that party, but I just had a couple hors d'oeuvres . . . well, maybe two little egg rolls, one little cheese pastry, a small handful of chips and salsa (you know, a full serving), and probably only six or seven little weenies. Oh, and that croissant . . ." *A boom chicka BOOM!*

There is some good news to this lesson, though: while a lot of a little negatives may equal a huge disaster, a lot of a little good things makes for a great success. After five years of teaching high school English, I put my career on hold to stay at home with my first child. One income couldn't cover all our expenses and leave us with any cushion, so I sold a product out of my home to supplement our income.

Over four short months, I found myself so successful

that I was on my way to earning a new car. At first it didn't seem attainable, but as the eighteen-month program arrived at its last month, it finally became real. Then again, so was the humongous sales goal my team had to make in that final month. As fate would have it, 70 percent of my team fell ill, most of my parties canceled, and I found myself faced with what seemed an insurmountable mountain to climb.

At about two-thirds of the way through the month and about one-quarter of the way to my goal, I called my mentor in tears. Our conversation not only changed the course of my month but also influenced how I would face uncountable other circumstances in my life. She said: "Amanda, how do you eat an elephant?"

Thinking this was some sort of silly joke, I just sat in silence.

Then she said, "One bite at a time. Have faith and ask God to guide you. Listen to all the seemingly silly little ideas, and follow the stirrings. This can still happen."

And you know what? All the small orders I got on the side, all the short phone calls I made, all the silly little ideas I had all came together to one amazing blessing. A lot of a little surely does equal a lot, which in my case was a shiny new Pontiac G6 hardtop convertible.

If you're facing what seems an insurmountable amount

of work, break it down into bite-sized tasks. Do the first thing first, then the next, and so on. Soon you'll be done and have more confidence for the next uphill climb.

Amanda Osburn has a bachelor's degree and teaching credential in English from California State University, Long Beach. She works as a high school English teacher and runs her own photography business.

GOD'S LIFE LESSON

All hard work brings a profit,
but mere talk leads only to poverty.

PROVERBS 14:23

LIVING THE LESSON

- Do a little something today that will help you on the road to accomplishing a larger task. For example, organize your paperwork into files.

- If you are job hunting, complete at least one job application each day this next week.

- Set SMART goals for your own personal growth—ones that are specific, measurable, attainable, relevant, and time bound.

- When you have a lot to accomplish, write down daily, specific tasks for the next day before going to bed. If they're written down, they won't keep you up at night, and you'll wake up the next day more task driven.

- Tell someone you trust what your goals are and how you're going to achieve them. That accountability will keep you more focused.

Quiet people have a lot to offer the world.

John Manion

I noticed something quickly when I started college. When everybody else left the dorm floors to go hang out at the beach or eat out, there were always a few individuals who stayed behind and kept to themselves. What I soon realized is that there's nothing wrong with these people. In fact, they have a lot to offer. So, I decided that I would stay behind occasionally and make it my mission to meet all the quiet, introverted people on my floor. Despite my own extroverted nature, two of them turned out to be future apartment-mates and my closest friends throughout college.

I was one of those guys who would move from room to room, planning group outings. However, I always had trouble getting one or two people to ever leave their rooms. One day I decided to try and get to know one of them—a quiet, Persian student named Shamim. Despite Shamim's quiet nature when in group settings, I discovered he could talk about intellectually stimulating topics for hours and surprisingly exhibited a comical personality. For the next four years, he was a study buddy, an apartment-mate, and one of my closest friends.

I've learned that it's important to have quiet people like this in your life: they can offer the deepest thoughts on important things. Besides, one day you might need someone to just sit in the same room with you who can keep his mouth shut for a little while.

John Manion is a graduate of University of California at Los Angeles with a BS in economics. He is serving his country as an officer in the US Army.

GOD'S LIFE LESSON

A friend loves at all times.

PROVERBS 17:17

LIVING THE LESSON

- When your extended family gets together, seek out the quiet relative and find out what he or she has been doing.

- Say a few kind words to the checkout clerk at the grocery the next time you're shopping.

- Avoid dominating the conversation with an introverted person. Ask interesting, open-ended questions that will draw the person out and show your interest in him or her. However, don't throw questions in a rapid-fire manner. It may be easier for a shy person to listen to you initially.

- Look for topics and activities that seem to interest the other person, such as a certain sports team or fiction genre.

- Invite that person to do something with you, such as see a new movie or get a cup of coffee.

Debt will chain you down.

Crystal Evans Walker

I received my very first credit card when I went to college and was so excited about that $200 credit limit! While I understood that whatever I charged I would have to pay back, I didn't understand that my credit limit would increase as I made my payments on time. Also, while I was aware that I was spending more than I was making in a month, I thought I was fine as long as I never missed the minimum payment.

Four years later, I had a degree in business and a job with an accounting firm. Two years after that, I married an awesome, godly man. However, while I loved numbers and created my own spreadsheets for our finances, there was a problem. The cost of living in southern California was high, and we had $20,000 in credit-card debt together.

We both worked overtime, but we still had barely enough money to pay those bills and student loans. Nevertheless, we bought our first house at the height of the real estate market and had our first child—and then my husband lost his job.

After a few more financial ups and downs, including a move to a more affordable area, we took an intense twelve-week financial class that helped us get back on track. We had several decisions to make. First, we put our credit cards away. Then my husband took on a second job, so I could homeschool our children. Lastly, we started our own health and wellness company. Gradually, we've paid off all our credit-card debt, my student loan, and my husband's student loan. We have been debt free now for over a year.

What I have learned from all this is that credit cards should only be a tool to build up your credit and make investments. Debt is serious, and it is not worth the cost. I would much rather save for what I want. It's better to wait. I've learned money is a tool to be used with caution. I've also learned not to rush into any big purchases. The biggest lesson is that God does not want us to be chained to debt, because money can cause stress on a marriage and even health problems. If we allow it to control us, it can separate us from God, too. I've learned to be content with what I have.

Crystal Walker has a degree in business administration with an emphasis in accounting from Biola University. She homeschools her children and works as a health and wellness consultant and sales representative.

GOD'S LIFE LESSON

Keep your lives free from the love
of money and be content with what
you have, because God has said,
"Never will I leave you;
never will I forsake you."

HEBREWS 13:5

LIVING THE LESSON

- Avoid debt by not carrying your credit cards in your wallet. In fact, cut them up or put them in a safe.

- If something is broken, try to fix it before buying a new one. Buy used items through thrift stores or Craigslist.

- Use the Thirty-Day Rule. Before you purchase something, wait thirty days to see if it is something you truly need or something you simply want.

- Write a list before you go grocery shopping and stick to it.

- Buy a good coffee maker instead of buying expensive drinks on a regular basis.

- Put some amount into savings each month—even if it's just five or ten dollars.

- Instead of adding expenses on a credit card for a trip, save up for it and look for good deals as you wait.

- Pay student loans faithfully. Not doing so will really hurt your credit score.

- Take a financial management course offered through a local college or your church.

There is value in understanding your personality.

Angelina Folchi

Throughout most of college, I compared myself to others and found my personality wanting. I determined that my brother, my boyfriend, and even fictional movie characters were doing life the right way—with lots of nonstop social activities—but I just couldn't. I enjoyed staying in and relaxing on weekend nights, but I felt like I *should* want to go out because that's what college students do. So, I thought there must be something wrong with me—that I was antisocial and distant. However, when I did force myself to socialize after a long week, I ended up exhausted and just did not have the energy I needed for the next full week of studies and work.

After a couple years of this internal conflict and a lot of emotional support from loved ones, I finally realized that I simply was an introverted person, someone who loses energy in social environments. I genuinely was wired differently from others around me, all of whom were extroverts—people who gain energy from being around others. Finally, I learned to just allow myself to recharge in my own quiet setting at the end of a stressful week. Resting, reading, and reflecting on a weekend help me ready myself for my week ahead—so that's what I still do.

Angelina Folchi graduated from the University of San Diego as a biology major and is presently working in research.

GOD'S LIFE LESSON

You created my inmost being;
you knit me together in my mother's womb.
I praise you because I am fearfully
and wonderfully made;
your works are wonderful,
I know that full well.

PSALM 139:13–14

LIVING THE LESSON

- Find out more about your personality type through the Myers and Briggs Foundation at www.myers-briggs.org.

- Create a weekly schedule for yourself that takes into consideration whether you are an introverted or extroverted person.

- Understand your personality's flaws, too, and then work toward making them strengths. For example, those with take-charge personalities tend to be leaders, but they can also be critical in nature. If you have a critical personality, work at encouraging others.

- Research jobs that tie to your personality type. People who are detail oriented, for example, are good at exacting work, such as engineering or accounting.

- After understanding the various personalities, recognize that each person is different and make strides toward accepting those differences.

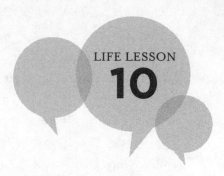

Respect builds
personal bridges.

Tyson Jaquez

I was blessed to have competed in Division I athletics. I learned a ton in my four years of college baseball, simply because playing sports at a high level is a lot like the game of life.

I was fortunate to play for a coach who was very strict and tough. He coached for thirty-three years at the Division I level, teaching hundreds of athletes. Almost all his former players are successful in life.

Little did I know while playing for him that he was preparing us for life. The most helpful lesson he taught me was to never burn bridges. I met and connected with many people in my four years in college who became bridges to a great career. I learned not to disappoint or let those people down, because then they lose trust in you. When they lose trust in you, that bridge is gone, and you cannot cross it again.

Since college I have worked for four different companies in sales. Because of the bridges that I formed in my college years, I have never had a real job interview and have always been hired on the spot. As the years go by, I just keep getting to know more great people and adding more bridges. I always keep in mind that I should treat others with respect so as to maintain our friendships—and the bridges that I may need to cross again someday.

Tyson Jaquez graduated from the University of Nevada, Reno, with a degree in sports physiology. He is a sales professional for an athletic gear company.

GOD'S LIFE LESSON

Live in harmony with one another.

ROMANS 12:16

LIVING THE LESSON

- Call an old friend you haven't heard from in a while.

- Make peace with someone you think harbors a grudge against you.

- Keep an awareness of your online persona. Avoid posting critical or embarrassing photos and comments that could alienate friends, family, and business contacts.

- Be genuine with people. While it is savvy to cultivate relationships for business purposes, you do not want people to feel as though you are using them for personal gain. Show sincere, personal interest in them.

- Share information with others when that could benefit them, such as a job notice that you feel is just right for someone.

A life's work should be meaningful.

Elizabeth Elorza

For a very long time, I chose the path of least resistance. It took a few missteps, but now I realize the importance of pursuing a career that is meaningful to me, not just easy. A path like that might be challenging, but it should have purpose and make me feel good about getting up in the morning.

After graduating from high school, I jumped into what I thought was the quickest and easiest program at the community college I chose to attend. I earned a degree in medical office administration. It wasn't long after I completed this program, however, that I realized I was not pursuing a profession that gave me joy and meaning. I had to admit to myself that I'd chosen one others had nudged me toward.

One day while watching my nephew, I looked at the eighteen-month-old strutting around and getting into everything, leaving messes in his wake. It was amazing how he had moved through so many developmental stages in just a short time. As he turned and smiled at me, I realized that working with children gave me much joy. I decided then that I wanted to work with children and started a job a short time later as a preschool teacher. That job convinced me to pursue studies to become an elementary school teacher. Fortunately, I was able to work as a high school aide while pursuing an online credential program on my off hours.

It took me many years to find my chosen path, but I have found a career that is meaningful to me . . . and it provides encouragement to others as well. We just have one life to live, so while it is important to be productive, it is critical to pursue a career that brings personal satisfaction.

Elizabeth Elorza graduated from Western Governors University with an interdisciplinary studies major. She is working as a high school instructional aide and softball coach until she can get a teaching position.

GOD'S LIFE LESSON

The LORD will fulfill his purpose for me.
LORD, your faithful love endures forever;
do not abandon the work of your hands.

PSALM 138:8 CSB

LIVING THE LESSON

- Think about what work would be meaningful to you, and create a ten-year plan for yourself.

- Email a mentor to thank him or her for nudging you down the right path.

- If you're confused about your future, think of five key words that would describe you—then try to tie them with careers.

- Consider meeting with a career coach who would ask questions about your passions, values, and talents and then help you discover a life path that you might not have otherwise considered.

- Think about this question: What work do you find yourself doing automatically? For example, if you naturally start thinking of ways to reorganize people's apartments, perhaps you would enjoy being an interior designer.

Success requires perseverance.

Christina Pasquetti Potter

Getting good grades in high school was easy for me. College, however, proved to be a bit different. While I didn't have to study so much in high school, studying in college was a daily occurrence. As a nursing major, I had to take anatomy and physiology, a very challenging course for me. I ended the semester with a C, but nursing school required at least a B in prerequisite courses. Frustrated, I decided I would change my major. However, when I sat down to pick courses in a new major, I realized that nursing was not only my major—it was my passion.

After thinking about this for a few days, I decided I needed to buck up, to learn to study better, and to retake the course. That was exactly what I did. I also enrolled in tutoring. Taking tutoring for the course was the best decision I made. It helped me not only with the course but in other classes as well. For the first time, I began understanding major concepts I would need for the practice of nursing, and I ended up getting an A. Not only that, I was asked to be on the dissection team and to tutor other students in that class.

From there, I finished my other nursing prerequisites and applied to my college's nursing program. I was accepted and graduated with honors. For the next five years, I worked as a registered nurse at a major hospital and then went on to graduate studies to become a family nurse practitioner. Had I not persevered with my course of study, I would not be where I am today. I had to work hard and apply myself; I couldn't just sit around wishing for things to happen or to come my way. Nursing was my passion from day one. It helps define who I am today, and it's what I love to do. I just had to do the hard work to make my dream come true.

Christina Potter graduated from the University of Nevada, Reno, with a degree in nursing and from the University of Nevada, Las Vegas, with a graduate degree as a family nurse practitioner. She is nationally certified in family practice.

GOD'S LIFE LESSON

Let us run with perseverance
the race marked out for us.

HEBREWS 12:1

LIVING THE LESSON

- Create a step-by-step plan for your life goal.

- Realistically identify potential obstacles as you work toward your goal, then seek out the support you will need to push through those challenges.

- Recognize that there will be critics who will try to drag you down, but do not let their negativity keep you from believing in yourself and your God-given abilities and passions.

- Understand that there are many fun distractions in life—social media, parties, television—but a greater enjoyment will be the satisfaction you have when you reach your goal.

- Don't compare yourself to others. Focus on your strengths and develop a determined mindset.

LIFE LESSON
13

Faith is a daily choice.

Weston Roberti

Raised in the Sierra Valley—an isolated, rural area of northern California—I did not realize how sheltered I had been from the rest of the world. However, as a freshman at Chico State, I soon noticed that the way I'd been raised was very uncommon compared to other students. This was most evident when it came to my Christian faith. The hardest thing for me during my college experience was finding a group of friends who believed what I believed and a church in which I could grow. The clear majority of young people around me did not attend church. Consequently, I struggled to pursue my faith.

I felt alone a lot. On Sundays, I went to church by myself or with maybe a friend or two that I'd convinced to accompany me. However, there were weekends when

51

I considered not going, when I wondered what was the point. One day, though, something clicked with me: following Jesus was a choice that I had to make on my own.

It had been easy to follow God when I was at home with my family encouraging me, but it was time for me to decide for myself if this was the life I wanted to follow. I had to decide if I wanted to follow Jesus, even though it was a lonely decision and it was easier to skip church to hang out with friends. How I was raised or what my family believed could not be my safety net. I had to decide personally to live out my faith. It was time to attend church and pursue my own spiritual growth through study and prayer because I wanted to, not because anyone else expected me to.

I now thank God for helping me make that decision during college. It led me to understand that a life of faith is the life I want to live. It is a choice I still make daily, but it is the best choice I ever made.

———————————

Weston Roberti graduated from California State University at Chico with a degree in agricultural science. He is pursuing a career as a cattle rancher on his family's large ranch.

GOD'S LIFE LESSON

If serving the LORD seems undesirable to you,
then choose for yourselves this day
whom you will serve . . . . But as for me
and my household, we will serve the LORD.

JOSHUA 24:15

LIVING THE LESSON

- Text or message a friend who could encourage you in your spiritual walk today or whom you yourself could encourage.

- If you haven't found a church home, commit to do so and do some online research of churches around you.

- Pray for the needs of your family and friends as they come to mind.

- Volunteer your time at your church—don't wait for someone to recruit you. Look for a need that matches your gifts and talents.

- Consider giving financially to your church.

You can pursue your relationship with God by reading the Bible.

Kelsey Scheckla

Looking back, I think others would say I was doing well. I had graduated from college, found a job that I enjoyed right away, and was in what I thought was a great relationship, but all that still was not enough for me. I thought I needed more. I constantly compared myself to others whose circumstances were completely different from mine, but I thought I should have what they had. I didn't recognize then that the vacuum in my life wasn't anything material—it was the need for a deeper relationship with God.

Encouraged by my family, I started an online read-through-the-Bible-in-a-year program but lost interest. The truth is, I had become complacent in personal aspects of my life, including my health and faith. Then one day I came across a blog on the Internet. The blogger focused mostly on prayer journaling and her journey with God. I immediately became hooked, researched what worked for her, and then branched out to other women to see what worked for them.

Bible journaling saved me. The fear, anxiety, and jealousy that had for many years paralyzed me vanished. My studies in the Bible gave me the insight and courage to free myself from a toxic relationship with a man. I learned not only how to talk with God, but also how to listen to Him and respect His plans for me. Journaling Bible verses—what they mean to me and how they affect my personal life—has showed me that the path I am on is mine and that I can overcome any challenge, fear, or doubt as long as my faith is strong and I listen closely to my Savior. Instead of looking to others for validation, I now know that I am valuable to the Lord of the universe—and my relationship with Him outweighs any other part of my life.

Kelsey Scheckla graduated from California State University at Fresno with a degree in animal science/livestock business management. Currently, she is working as a veterinary technician in a veterinary center.

GOD'S LIFE LESSON

Your word is a lamp for my feet,
a light on my path.

PSALM 119:105

LIVING THE LESSON

- Write out sticky notes with Bible verses that have encouraged you over the years and place them where you will see them.

- Decide on a Bible-reading plan—what you will read and when—that is realistic for your schedule. Try using a highlighter or pen to mark verses that especially speak truth to you for the present circumstances of your life.

- Find someone older in the faith who would meet with you on a regular basis to teach and mentor you.

- Seek out a fellowship group that will help you grow in the faith.

- Check out the new journaling Bibles that provide opportunities for you to meditate on the Word as you artistically represent the Scriptures.

Engaging with others demonstrates your care for them.

Aaron Boigon

My grandfather, Harold, is a legend in my family for having brought so many smiles to so many faces. Whether talking to family, friends, or complete strangers, he always elicited the most genuine smiles. You know the kind—smiles that produce delightful creases and twinkling eyes. I didn't understand the power of this until I attended college, encountering the world on my own for the first time.

One afternoon I was at the student services office talking to an administrator, trying to sort out a problem caused by a glitch in the school's system. The stony-faced administrator didn't make things easy, but I was determined to make her smile and engage on a more personal level. And then I thought about my grandpa. My grandfather genuinely cared about people. He asked questions, he listened, and he made lots of disarming little jokes—in short, he *delighted* them. This, I realized, was the power of mirth. By bringing levity and delight—by truly engaging in conversation—I too could win people over.

With that thought, I started asking questions and learned the administrator had been dealing with angry students all day, thanks to the computer glitch. I won her over when I quipped, "Well . . . look on the bright side: this postpones the rise of the machines against humanity by at least one more day, right?" She chuckled, told me she would personally see to it the problem was fixed that day, and then called me directly an hour later to confirm.

I've put this principle into practice every day since by making it a point to be fully present when I'm talking with other people so I can try to see the world through their eyes. No matter the situation, this approach never fails to find the quickest path to compassion and connectedness.

Aaron Boigon graduated from the University of Washington with degrees in philosophy and comparative history. He currently works as a senior vice president and director of information technology at a community bank.

GOD'S LIFE LESSON

Now we ask you, brothers and sisters,
to acknowledge those who work hard
among you, who care for you
in the Lord and who admonish you.
Hold them in the highest regard
in love because of their work.
Live in peace with each other.

1 THESSALONIANS 5:12–13

LIVING THE LESSON

- The next time you are at the grocery store, ask your checker, "Do you like your job?"

- When you speak to customer service representatives on the phone, put yourself in their shoes. Pay attention to your tone of voice, and let them know you appreciate their help.

- When you meet someone for the first time, look that person in the eyes, smile, and shake hands firmly.

- Hold the door open for those older than you as you enter a building.

- The next time you're stuck in a line, see it as an opportunity to engage the people around you in conversation. Here's a good opener: "Have you always lived in the area?"

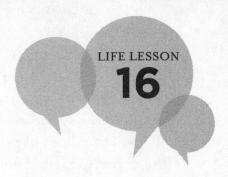

You don't have to win every argument.

Amanda Page

I grew up in a small, predominantly conservative, rural town, where gossip flies faster than a june bug on a hot summer day and your closest neighbor is probably a distant relative of some sort. I'm sure you can imagine my state of shock when I arrived in the San Francisco Bay Area for my first day of college at a liberal, all-women's school, where I knew absolutely no one. As a frantic freshman trying to find her way around campus, I was busy gawking at the people with crazy hairdos, eccentric outfits, and awkwardly placed piercings . . . among other things. I also learned that some of these people had very different morals, values, opinions, and cultural beliefs—differences that would challenge me over the next four years.

The most valuable thing I learned while in school (and something that has far outlasted any psychology vocabulary or statistics equation) is the art of knowing how to respect others' differences—specifically, how to agree to disagree cohesively. I learned to pick my battles instead of allowing myself to be drawn into heated debates, after which both parties leave feeling unsatisfied and unvindicated.

If something didn't directly affect my health, well-being, or safety, I learned to let it go. I would leave the conversation, change the topic, nod in agreement while gritting my teeth—essentially I looked the other way. This tactic has saved many friendships and allows me to maintain respectful relationships with many people from all walks of life. Doing this taught me a lot about people, places, and the world in general; I've become a more knowledgeable, well-rounded person.

Despite significant differences in lifestyles and choices, I found that those moments of self-controlled disagreement gave me the opportunity to share my ideas and beliefs. Respectful disagreement allows me to make a positive impression and potentially influence others. I've discovered that I can stand firm in who I am and what I represent, while still demonstrating understanding and respect for others through empathy and compassion. In that way, others of different backgrounds did not feel shut out or ignored.

Amanda Page graduated from Mills College in Oakland, where she majored in psychology. She currently works as an education and outreach director for the US Department of Defense.

GOD'S LIFE LESSON

Accept one another, then,
just as Christ accepted you,
in order to bring praise to God.

ROMANS 15:7

LIVING THE LESSON

- Think about your objective—do you simply want to share your ideas, or do you hope to convince the other person to agree with you?

- When someone expresses an opinion, use the art of reiteration by saying, "What I hear you saying is . . . ." Then finish the sentence by summarizing what that person said.

- Think about your demeanor and tone of voice during a discussion. Shift from a snarl to a slight smile and from a raised voice to a calm, respectful one.

- Be careful not to insult others or use name-calling or stereotyping when sharing your viewpoints. Decide not to become offended by someone else's ideas.

- If a discussion becomes heated, take a deep breath and say, "While I don't agree with what you've said, I appreciate the opportunity to discuss this with you."

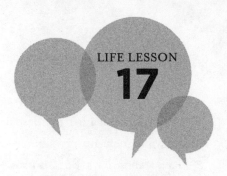

Tolerance is putting yourself in someone else's shoes.

Benakar Batista

My dad was a diplomat for several African countries, and the most important lesson he taught me while growing up was tolerance for others. The easiest way I found to do that was to put myself in the other person's shoes. I have tried my best to live by that rule every day with all my interactions, particularly the difficult ones. Fourteen years ago, I painfully added an additional layer of understanding.

My dad was diagnosed with a terminal illness. The news caught my family by surprise and crushed us. I well remember the bare hospital hallways where my family and I paced up and down all day, waiting for the doctor to give us a glimpse of hope. However, for whatever reason, the doctor was unreachable—too busy to give us an update.

Today, as a physician, I do perhaps understand why the doctor might have been so evasive. Maybe he just couldn't face us. I remember the despair in my mom's eyes and the bewilderment on my siblings' faces. It still hurts to think about those days. But I promised myself that I would never forget that pain, that I would care for patients and their family and always take time to explain their situation. Whether they have a cold or an ominous ailment, people are at their most vulnerable when they are ill. Every time I put myself in my patient's shoes—every time I am patient, kind, and accessible—I aim to give others that glimpse of hope that I yearned for so many years ago. If we all could learn to empathize with others, we would find that we have more in common than surface differences would otherwise indicate.

Benakar Batista earned a bachelor's degree in biology from Northeastern University and a medical doctor's degree from University of Connecticut. She works as an OB/GYN physician, formerly for the US Army.

GOD'S LIFE LESSON

Love your neighbor as yourself.

MARK 12:31

LIVING THE LESSON

- If someone is responding negatively toward you, pause and look pleasantly at that person before you respond.

- Think about a similar frustration or hurt you have had and say, "How could I help you?"

- Recognize that you can change your soft skills (interactions with other people).

- When someone is speaking, practice active listening instead of thinking about what your next response will be.

- Validate the other person's perspective by saying, "I can see why you would be frustrated."

Confidence is key.

Kyle Jaquez

Growing up in a town with less than one thousand people and going to school with fewer than fifty other kids made me feel outnumbered and insecure when I went away to college. I thought that I hadn't been taught half as much as what others had learned in their big city schools. I was an athlete, too, playing baseball for the school. My insecurities affected me all around. I was always second-guessing what I should do or say, whether it was a cutoff drill during infield practice or math formulas in the class-room. It cost me playing time, and it made me overthink some of my schoolwork. I finally figured out the key in my senior year.

I was warming up in the bullpen at an away game at Cal Poly, Pomona. It was the seventh inning, and the pitcher—one of my best friends—was in trouble. He had walked a couple guys, and then the next batter hit a single up the middle to load the bases. My team from Menlo College had only one out.

I was always jittery before I went in as a relief pitcher, plagued by the same butterflies-in-your-stomach feeling that often affected my schoolwork. That day, however, I was determined I would do my best. I decided confidence was the key and put one foot in front of the other as the coach waved me in.

I reminded myself how hard I had practiced and worked for this moment. *You can do this. Trust your ability. Whatever happens, happens.* I kept the talk going in my head.

The first batter flew out. Two outs.

The next batter grounded out to third base. *I did it!* Three outs.

As I walked off the mound that inning, my pitching coach said, "Way to look like you've been there before."

From that point on—whether in baseball back then or in the business world now—I have remembered the lesson I learned in that game: prepare well and step out confidently.

Kyle Jaquez graduated from Menlo College in Atherton, California, with a degree in business management. He is currently working as a financial consultant with an investment company.

GOD'S LIFE LESSON

I can do all this through him
who gives me strength.

PHILIPPIANS 4:13

LIVING THE LESSON

- When faced with an important meeting, groom yourself and dress the part. Professional business attire can boost your confidence.

- Think positively. Memorize the verse on the previous page and know that you have the personal strength to get through the challenge ahead.

- If you tend to be introverted and get butterflies when you speak in public, simply pretend you're not. Look people in the eyes, smile, and greet them warmly.

- Treat others as you would like to be treated—first, because it's the right thing to do, and second, because others will react to you more positively.

- Be prepared. If you haven't done your figurative (or literal) homework, you will not be as confident going into the situation ahead.

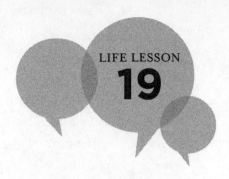

Others' perspectives are valuable for problem solving.

Steven Martinez

I t is important to know what you believe and where you stand on important matters. However, to navigate through the complexities and practicalities of daily life—school, work, home—I have learned that holding fast to only my own opinions limits my interactions and relationships with others.

I cannot recall the exact moment when I learned to listen to and value other people's ideas. I think it was more of an intuitive nudge before it became a conscious effort. However, an audiobook I once listened to outlined the process of problem solving through empathy and challenged me to work actively to understand another's point of view.

The fact is, most everyone we interact with has a set of opinions that can parallel perfectly with or skew widely from our own. I'm most often reminded of this in group settings, like a collaborative project or a critical meeting in my engineering firm. At these times, it is important to listen, ask, empathize, reframe, and strategize—not only to keep the peace but also to come to the best possible outcome. While not abandoning my own convictions, ideas, or beliefs, I can demonstrate value for others' perspectives. By not alienating the other person, I have found we can come to a mutually agreeable solution to a problem. The compromise is not a defeat; conversely, the victory is our developing a solution where there had been none.

Steven Martinez has a degree in mechanical engineering from the University of California, Berkeley, and works as a mechanical engineer.

GOD'S LIFE LESSON

Love . . . does not boast,
it is not proud.
It does not dishonor others,
it is not self-seeking.

1 CORINTHIANS 13:4–5

LIVING THE LESSON

- Ask the others in your work meeting what they think the problem or obstacle is.

- Then ask them what their solution would be for solving the problem or eliminating the obstacle.

- If you are in a business meeting, take notes as your colleagues share their ideas. This practice may help you see their ideas more objectively.

- Respond to others' comments first by summarizing what they have said: "What I heard you say was . . . ."

- Create pros and cons lists for each of the solutions, incorporating input from the group.

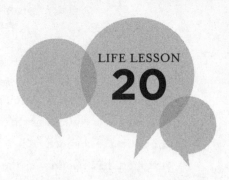

We have much to learn from the elderly.

Brittany Keep

I was too young to appreciate how valuable my time was with my only grandparent until it was too late. I now regret not taking the time to help my grandma and to truly listen to her.

However, over the past year and a half, I have had the pleasure of helping to care for an eighty-four-year-old widower named Robert. My time with him has proven more valuable to me than I ever thought it would be. During the evenings when we sit down to eat, we talk about anything and everything. He tells me the stories of his life, and I listen intently to every word. He lights up every time he shares his memories and experiences with me.

I have learned so much about life, love, and hardships

by listening to him. More importantly, though, I have seen how much just having someone there makes a difference for him. Just the other night, he hugged me tightly and told me how lucky he was that I had come into his life—but I know I'm the lucky one.

Robert has taught me the importance of extending grace to others in this world. Elderly people still have a lot to offer those willing to spend the time with them. I have learned how significant it is for elderly people to know that there is still someone who values their time and the knowledge they have to offer. Life is short. Spend some quality time with your grandparents; learn from their life experience.

———————————————

Brittany Keep has a bachelor's degree in animal science from California State University, Chico. She currently is the foster coordinator at an animal shelter.

GOD'S LIFE LESSON

Do not cast me away when I am old;
do not forsake me when
my strength is gone.

PSALM 71:9

LIVING THE LESSON

- Write regular snail-mail letters or postcards to your living grandparents.

- Call an elderly person you love and get caught up on their lives.

- Visit your local convalescent hospital occasionally; even quick visits are appreciated.

- Write down your grandparents' stories and compile them for your family.

- Create special memories by taking an older family member on a day trip someplace he or she would like to visit.

Real friends speak the truth in love.

Teagan Thompson Greenwood

The most trusted people in my life are those who have been bold enough to lovingly speak the truth to me when they felt I wasn't making the best choices.

One day when I was in college, my best friend came to me regarding some new "friends" I had started investing in. These people liked going out and staying up late which was fine for them because they weren't in school. I was, however, and my grades started to slip because I was too tired to make it to class and was neglecting my homework. If she hadn't spoken up when she did, I probably would have dropped or failed classes I needed to complete. While it was hard to hear my friend question my behavior at the time, I now see how hard my life could have been had she not intervened.

I am so thankful that over the years, people have loved and cared for me enough to shine light on the darkness of my bad decisions. Speaking the truth isn't always the easiest thing to do, especially when it comes to people you love and don't want to hurt. It is certainly not comfortable to tell someone, "Hey, because I love you, I'm concerned about your drinking," or "I care about you, and I think that person doesn't really have your best interests at heart." But speaking the truth *in love* will benefit all parties involved.

When a person loves you enough to tell you the truth, humble yourself to listen. Real friendships are those where you care enough for people that you tell them the truth in a loving way—even when doing so means you risk making them angry or maybe even risk losing the friendship altogether. Real friends care that much.

Teagan Greenwood has a degree in human development and family studies from the University of Nevada, Reno. She worked as a teacher for several years before she decided to stay home as a full-time mother.

GOD'S LIFE LESSON

Speaking the truth in love,
we will grow to become in every respect
the mature body of him
who is the head, that is, Christ.

EPHESIANS 4:15

LIVING THE LESSON

- If a friend or family member challenges you about your negative behavior, listen to his or her concerns without becoming defensive.

- If you see a friend making poor decisions that will lead to self-sabotage, look for the right setting for that conversation—one that is private, where both parties can be relaxed. Pray for the right place and timing.

- In that conversation, choose a very specific issue to discuss; don't bring in peripheral issues that will cloud the conversation.

- Have a thoughtful card prepared for the person— a thinking-of-you card—with a pertinent Scripture verse and your own words of friendship.

- Set another time with that person to have coffee or lunch. This will show that you care about the relationship and are willing to be a true friend.

Traveling will broaden your outlook.

Katie Roberti

When I was ten years old, my family went on a mission trip to Tecate, Mexico. I vividly remember that cherished adventure. When we drove back across the border into California, I had not only a new perspective of the people of Mexico but also an understanding of the contrasting lifestyle Americans typically live. This trip lit a spark in me to travel, but more importantly to interact with people around the world and understand other cultures.

Fast-forward a decade . . . travel remained at the top of my interests throughout college. I took every opportunity possible to explore new areas and take advantage of student discounts. Through internships, trips to conferences with campus clubs, and spontaneous getaways with friends, I was able to travel often and affordably during my four years at Cal Poly, San Luis Obispo.

The summer before my senior year, I studied in London. I learned not all classrooms have four walls. Exploring the streets of London and traveling on the weekends, I met people from across the world. Quickly, I found out that although no two cultures are the same, we all have more in common than we think.

It takes hard work and financial sacrifice to make travel happen, but the joy and new knowledge I have each time I board my return flight make it all worthwhile. College was the best four years of my life thus far, and much of that is credited to being able to see so much of the world and experience how God has uniquely created each person in every culture.

Katie Roberti has a degree in agricultural communication from California Polytechnic State University, San Luis Obispo, and a master's degree in media innovation from the University of Nevada, Reno. She is currently working for a agricultural nonprofit organization.

GOD'S LIFE LESSON

From one man he made all the nations,
that they should inhabit the whole earth;
and he marked out their appointed times
in history and the boundaries of their lands.

ACTS 17:26

LIVING THE LESSON

- Save enough in one year for a trip abroad by eliminating these money-eaters: cable or satellite TV, expensive coffee drinks, expensive haircuts, and gym or spa memberships.

- Investigate these resources for a trip overseas: education-abroad programs, Groupon tours, travel bloggers, travel agents, and online services such as Costcotravel.com.

- Consider getting a passport so you have the flexibility to take advantage of overseas deals. You can start the process online at https://travel.state.gov/. Avoid using a private processor, because this will just cost you more money and may not be reliable.

- If you're planning to travel, call your bank and credit card companies so they know you will be using your cards.

- When you fly, carry a change of clothes and necessities in your carry-on luggage in case your checked luggage doesn't arrive on time.

Life isn't fair.

Leah Warren

Life isn't fair." Most of us have heard some version of that refrain for much of our lives through movies (*Princess Bride*, anyone? "Life isn't fair. It's just fairer than death, that's all"), television shows, and even older family members. It's been hammered home as we've had to contend with crippling student debt, a tough job market, steep housing prices, and a tense political atmosphere, all of which leave us feeling unheard.

It was shortly after graduation that I realized focusing on life's seeming injustices was killing me—perhaps not physically, but definitely spiritually. As I was browsing my corner of the Internet, I stumbled across the saying, "You cannot control other people's actions, only the situations you put yourself in." That resonated with me, because I don't react well when other people's actions force me to alter my plans. I'd much rather be in complete control. I've had to learn how to refocus on the situations and issues I actually have a say in—usually my own actions and attitudes more than other people's. Unsurprisingly, my stress levels have since dropped, and I'm becoming a more adaptive person. Humorously enough, the more flexible I become, the less unfair life seems.

Yes, life isn't fair, but what do we mean when we say that? That someone else has easier access to better opportunities than we do? That someone in authority acted unethically, and that person's actions hurt us? These are not situations we can control, and that's probably why we resent them so. Ultimately, life is a far more enjoyable adventure when we focus on overcoming its challenges, rather than whether those challenges should even exist. Life will never be fair, but that doesn't mean it will never be fulfilling.

Leah Warren has a degree in English literature from Sonoma State University and works as a nanny and in her church office.

GOD'S LIFE LESSON

He has shown you, O mortal, what is good.
And what does the LORD require of you?
To act justly and to love mercy
and to walk humbly with your God.

MICAH 6:8

LIVING THE LESSON

- Write letters of encouragement to members of the military serving overseas or in VA hosptials.

- Organize a group of people to serve meals in a homeless shelter.

- Volunteer as a coach at your local Boys and Girls Club or teen centers.

- Consider becoming a Big Brother or Big Sister through the Big Brothers Big Sisters of America organization.

- Donate time as a children's teacher at your local church.

Be thankful for something every day.

Elizabeth McDermott

There are days it's easy to be thankful. Maybe you're thankful for a new degree, a new job, loving family and friends, or even the cup of tea that will see you through the next hour. Some days, though, it's harder to find a grateful attitude. On those days, perhaps more than any other, it's important to find something to be thankful for. Anything. Even if all you see around you is shadows, thank God for them, because their existence means His light is shining just around the corner.

Some years ago, my husband and I lived on a rural Idaho mountain with two young children. His parents and seven siblings lived on the property next to ours, and when a mudslide threatened their home, they sought refuge with us. Overnight, I faced the challenge of thirteen people in my house—an adventure that lasted five months. Nonetheless, I made a conscious decision in the midst of that living situation to wake up each morning with one primary mission: find something today to be thankful for.

Some days it was simple. *Thank You, God, for help in the kitchen today.* Some days it was a little more exciting. *Thank You, God, for keeping us all safe in the lightning storm.* However, there were days I didn't want to be thankful, and those days the frustrations and stresses crept eagerly into my heart. They threatened my patience and tried my self-control, but I knew that a negative attitude wouldn't help anybody, so I thanked God instead for strength to get out of the mire. My home is once again my own, but I still wake up looking for things to be grateful for. If a thankful outlook can bring peace in times of chaos, imagine what it can do in everyday life.

Elizabeth McDermott graduated from Sonoma State University with a degree in English with an emphasis in creative writing. Currently, she is a stay-at-home mom of five.

GOD'S LIFE LESSON

Rejoice always, pray continually,

give thanks in all circumstances;

for this is God's will for you

in Christ Jesus.

1 THESSALONIANS 5:16–18

LIVING THE LESSON

- Keep a journal of thanks—write down one thing, situation, or person that you are thankful for each day.

- When you're having a particularly hard day, read through your journal to see how you have been blessed.

- Rethink how you appear on social media. If you're constantly posting your issues, you aren't demonstrating a thankful attitude.

- Thank someone today for how he or she has helped you.

- Read the book *One Thousand Gifts* by Ann Voskamp, who helps the reader be thankful in the midst of heartache.

Every day is worth cherishing.

Whitney Adams May

I have a very distinct memory from my first year in college—I was hanging out in my dorm room with my roommate and telling her about how I couldn't wait to be done with college and to move out of the dorms. I was ready to be "grown up and on my own." My roommate was kind of shocked: "You don't think you're going to miss this?" While I quickly dismissed her comment, she reassured me that I would look back fondly on my college days. Boy, was she right, and I ever so wrong!

Fast-forward eleven years. I am in that stage I longed for in college: happily married with two kids, a house, and a rewarding career. But I find myself wondering why my nineteen-year-old self was in such a rush. While my current stage of life is truly all I had hoped for, so were my college years. Each chapter of our lives has value and teaches us something. I have learned to cherish every stage and every single living moment, because each goes by quickly.

While we all say, "I can't wait until . . . ," I realized I was wishing some of my life away. What about those moments in between those events—each of which has value? Even now, when I want my workweek to be over to spend the weekend with my babies, I remind myself that those moments at work matter, too. Every day matters and has value.

Though not every day brings us sheer happiness, it is another day we get to live and enjoy all that is around us. It's easy to get caught up in life and wish for the next big moment, but I encourage you not to wish your life away. If we pause occasionally, we can notice the small circumstances of daily living that bring us joy—a child's laugh, the sun peeking through the clouds, a sip of great coffee, a job well done—so that we can enjoy every bit of life we are given.

Whitney May is a kinesiology graduate of San Diego State University, as well as a graduate from University of California at Davis School of Medicine's physician assistant program. She works in primary care as a physician assistant.

GOD'S LIFE LESSON

———————————————

The LORD has done it this very day;
let us rejoice today and be glad.

PSALM 118:24

LIVING THE LESSON

- Instead of allowing traffic to bother you as you drive, use the time to appreciate your surroundings. Also, instead of leaving for your destination at the last possible moment, allow yourself extra time in case there are delays.

- When someone is speaking to you, focus solely on that person: look at him or her intently and listen without thinking ahead to how you will respond.

- Rather than seeing your daily tasks as a means to the end, be more mindful as you are working. See your work as your best offering to your employer and coworkers.

- Determine to be a blessing to someone today. Give a compliment. Share a funny story. Be the person who will turn a negative vibe into a positive one.

- Notice something spectacular today about the nature around you—how the moon creeps up from the horizon, the fresh smell after a rain, a flower in a sidewalk crack.

People are more valuable than things.

Selina R. Melancon

Although my parents always set an example of living simply, when I was at my first job out of college and making a full-time salary, I developed a love for shopping. For me, the pursuit of material things was driven by a question that had always burned in my heart, "Lord, am I beautiful?" Instead of awaiting His answer, I bought things. Dresses. Jewelry. High heels. Boots. Handbags. Expensive hair products. And always a new makeup experiment—the more expensive, the greater its promise . . . but the greater the disappointment when I looked more or less the same. The trouble was that I was never satisfied; I shopped, not so much for what I really needed, but in an effort to look as good as or better than others.

One day, I read a quote from St. John Paul II that said we don't *have* a body or *have* a soul: rather a human person *is* a body and equally *is* a soul. It struck me that my quest for happiness by way of buying things only involved half of my person, and the other half of my person suffered as a result. I was inspired to bring balance into my life, to seek the beauty of my soul in addition to the beauty of my body. This manifested itself in many ways as I began to walk in a new direction, but there is one weekend I will never forget.

One of my dearest friends came to visit, and it struck me that I had always envied her. For the first time, I saw an invisible wall between us that I had built. I said, "I'm downsizing my wardrobe. Please go shopping! Have fun!"

She looked a little skeptical. "What if I pick *your* favorite thing and take it?"

Without thinking, I said, "If there is a single thing in this closet that has such a grip on me I would refuse it to my dearest friend, that's the thing I *most* want out of my life."

She looked around at everything and finally pointed to a black handbag with a gold zipper. She said with a smile, "I always loved this one." With bursting joy, I put it in her hands.

While outwardly nothing had changed, I felt free. My possessions no longer had power over me. A weight I didn't know I had been carrying was removed. This sense of detachment brought a powerful joy. While we selfishly guard the things in our lives we believe will make us happy, grasping at them and refusing to share, God invites us to offer everything to Him. For the first time, I knew with certainty that I valued my friend more than anything material I owned.

Selina Melancon has a degree in English from the University of Nevada, Las Vegas. She works for a nonprofit social service agency.

GOD'S LIFE LESSON

Where your treasure is,
there your heart will be also.

MATTHEW 6:21

LIVING THE LESSON

- Practice detachment in small things: give away that last piece of cake you were saving for yourself or buy a necklace you love and give it to a friend or sister instead.

- Choose one expensive makeup or hair product you will do without and use the money you save to give hope to a child in need.

- Look at your things, one by one. If they do not give you joy or provide meaning to your life, allow them to give joy or meaning to someone else—either by giving them away or selling them at a yard sale. Yard sale proceeds could be used to pay off debt or help someone in need.

- Check out Project 333 online—a suggestion that you dress with only thirty-three items for three months.

- If you're spending time with a friend, turn your cell phone off completely and appreciate the gift of time your friend is giving you.

Asking significant questions can lead to truth.

Bethany McHenry Mariconda

In my final semester of college I was inspired to learn. I can't remember why I signed up for a class called the Geography of the Imagination, but the man teaching it forever changed the way I speak, read, and think.

All the professor did was invite me into a conversation. Each week, he required his students to read a book and then come to class to talk about what we thought of it. There was no threaded theme to the texts we read, but all were stories written by people attempting to share truth about a subject. The class would gather around an oval table once a week and wait for our professor's question: "Be honest. What was your experience reading the book this week?" With pages of notes, my peers would come to class loving the book, hating the book, or questioning the author's intentions.

My professor would sit, listen, and ask clarifying questions to be sure he truly understood each individual's stance. Then he would ask significant questions about our reading experiences. He valued every word we spoke and took time to address each question, concern, and tangent. It was poetry to listen to him conduct a conversation and get truth out of us simply by asking us to re-explain something, build on an idea we had shared, or make a personal connection. Because of his significant questions, I listened to personal stories I never would have heard and developed relationships I never would have given a chance.

Each class we attended created an opportunity for honesty, connection, healing, perspective, humility, purpose, vulnerability, and trust. Around that table, my professor built a community as we pursued learning together. It took me most of the semester to realize that the class was never about dissecting arguments; it was about learning to honor other people by asking significant questions. Ultimately, that book club professor inspired me to learn, to care, and to teach others to do the same.

Bethany Mariconda graduated from the University of California, Berkeley, with a degree in rhetoric. She is pursuing a master's degree at the University of Hawaii and is teaching high school English.

GOD'S LIFE LESSON

You will know the truth,
and the truth will set you free.

JOHN 8:32

LIVING THE LESSON

- As you meet people, take time to listen to their stories.

- In your conversations, challenge yourself to ask questions that go beyond superficial levels. These could include the following: "Why did you decide to go into teaching?" "What do you value in a friendship?" "What is your greatest personal need right now?"

- As deeper conversations usually do not happen in minutes-long encounters, schedule time with friends and family that will allow discussions to go more deeply than surface levels.

- Start a monthly book club. Often the questions related to a book focus on important life issues.

- Churches often have small groups that meet to discuss the weekly message. Find one and join the conversation.

Change brings opportunities for growth.

Carolyn Ule

When I was in high school, I believed I was at the pinnacle of my life—that there was no direction but down from that peak of my existence. Consequently, when I went to college, I clung desperately to my old friends and patterns, afraid to abandon the idyllic memories of my youth. However, one day a good friend questioned my nostalgia and despondent attitude.

That was a wake-up call. She was right. While I had formerly been a go-getter who always looked for adventure and typically pushed for the sky, I had to admit that my life had stagnated. Maybe it would be okay to embrace the people and situations in my present life. Perhaps these steps into my future were not as dim and empty as I had thought.

I determined to embrace change; after all, to change means you become something different, not necessarily something worse. I decided that day to say yes to any new activities I was invited to participate in. Consequently, I encountered a variety of new ideas and learned to examine concepts from multiple angles. My world began to broaden beyond those comfortable walls. Change was not leaving an idyllic existence—it was the embrace of something potentially better than I had already experienced.

People say the years of youth are the best years of your life, but if you embrace change and live fully, every year can be the best year of your life. Change is just a new opportunity to grow into the person you want to be. Staying positive as your life changes allows you to embrace the best of a new situation, and that will help you achieve the long-term goals that you have for yourself. I now know that, as good as my memories are, my best years are always the ones ahead of me.

Carolyn Ule has a degree in cellular and developmental biology from University of California, Santa Barbara. Currently, she is working on a master's degree in global medicine at the University of Southern California while she works as an EMT in Los Angeles.

GOD'S LIFE LESSON

Be strong and courageous.
Do not be afraid; do not be discouraged,
for the LORD your God will be
with you wherever you go.

JOSHUA 1:9

LIVING THE LESSON

- Before you move to a new area, ask people who have visited there or currently live there what they like most about the area.

- As you move to a new location, visit the local restaurants and coffee shops to people watch. Smile a lot. Engage someone in conversation. Make a new friend.

- Ask people you meet for interesting places in the area. Create a Google Doc or Google Map and invite others to collaborate on the project.

- Continue a hobby you've always pursued. If you snowboard, for example, you're likely to meet others who do.

- Volunteer for a charity event, such as a 3K/5K race for a cancer organization. You'll meet people and help the cause.

You can learn from every person you meet.

Zachariah Manion

The average person will interact with eighty thousand people in their lifetime. What if every single person had something valuable to give? How rich could you be with that much education?

Several years ago, an arrogant, confrontational manager started leading my department at the company where I worked in China. He was condescending and demeaning. Within a week, he fired seven out of the ten colleagues on our team whose previous performance had been less than spectacular, and soon thereafter, even those who survived the cutbacks quit. After a year, I was the only person left on the team, and I was ready to give up on a future at the company. I informed the chief executive officer of the company that I was looking for a new job and would be leaving. While he admitted that he had made a mistake in hiring the manager, he said, "Zak, learn something from every person you ever meet."

What I eventually learned through that manager's negative example was what *not* to do—how not to treat people. I was in that toxic environment for a year, but I stuck it out, studied the situation, and worked hard to learn what I could do if I were given the opportunity. And I was. When the manager failed his annual goals, he was moved to the back office, and I was given the team.

I stayed with that company and went on to have my proudest moments. With that in mind, I have discovered I can learn something from everyone I encounter. Strangers and acquaintances. Enemies and friends. Beggars and philanthropists. Haters and kind people. Television personalities and colleagues. Each person has a valuable lesson, be it negative or positive.

All people we encounter can teach us something through what they say and how they behave. Of course, that means that you have something to teach and give as well.

Zachariah Manion graduated from Pepperdine University with a degree in economics. He works as a marketing analyst in China for an international advertising agency.

GOD'S LIFE LESSON

So in everything, do to others
what you would have them do to you,
for this sums up the Law and the Prophets.

MATTHEW 7:12

LIVING THE LESSON

- Be courteous to others in traffic; we all make mistakes.

- Be friendly and kind to those who serve you, such as waiters and hotel maids.

- Learn from others' mistakes. They can save you heartache if you decide not to do what they did.

- Read nonfiction books on leadership. These often convey a lot of business helps and keep you apprised of current management philosophies and strategies.

- Thank the positive role models in your life for teaching you practical life skills.

Your health is important.

Maddi Morris

In the beginning of my college career, I was a bit over-weight and obsessed over my body and my lack of results, even though I was working out often. I became increasingly unhappy. However, as I pursued my college studies in kinesiology, I began to embrace what my professors taught me—that health requires balance. Wellness involves more than the physical body; our mental state and emotions are part of the picture, too.

My new understanding of wellness settled over me in several ways. First, I realized I didn't have to kill myself in the gym; exercising several times a week for thirty to sixty minutes a session was enough. I also learned to find activities that I liked, such as hiking, so that working out didn't seem like a chore. Then I found that eating well made me feel well and helped me achieve better results.

I stopped using food as a reward and indulging in what I had considered "treat meals." (These were actually punishment, because they made me feel worse.) Finally, I began to use positive self-talk when I looked in the mirror. Once I became comfortable with the process and stopped obsessing with day-to-day results or mistakes, I was able to achieve personal health goals and feel good about myself again.

Our health is important; it gives us life and vitality. In a class I took called Exercise Prescription for Chronic Illnesses, I found that many of the illnesses we associate with aging are preventable by simply eating well and living an active life. Getting strong now is important so we can experience amazing hikes to incredible views, so we can run and play endlessly with our children, and so we can provide for our family and friends. If you love the ocean, pursue scuba diving as a pastime. If you like an adrenaline high, take up rock climbing. If you love looking at beautiful landscapes, walk to one and recreate it on canvas with paints. Finding and pursuing an active, fulfilling life will make you more attractive and more content.

Maddi Morris has a degree in kinesiology with an emphasis in exercise and fitness from San Jose State University. She is currently self-employed as a wellness coach and health-supplements distributor.

GOD'S LIFE LESSON

Physical training is of some value,
but godliness has value for all things,
holding promise for both
the present life and the life to come.

1 TIMOTHY 4:8

LIVING THE LESSON

- Keep a food journal, not to count calories but to be aware of the types of food you consume on a regular basis so you can cut those foods that do not align with your goals.

- Avoid fad diets. Instead, consume a daily balance of healthy foods: protein, vegetables, fruits, whole grains, and healthy fats.

- Invest in an activity tracker to monitor your activity levels.

- Balance your exercise with cardio and strength training activity. Always include stretching after your body has warmed up about five minutes into your exercise and after you finish your workout.

- Stay hydrated by drinking half your weight in ounces. For example, a 150-pound person should first drink at least 75 ounces of water first each day, then consume other drinks.

- Get between seven and nine hours of sleep each night. Cutting yourself short on sleep could lead to a weakened immune system, meaning you could get sick more easily.

Procrastination only creates more pressure.

Amonie Snodgrass Keller

I've always been both a perfectionist and a procrastinator. My first college attempt was right after high school. I had no idea what I wanted to do and, two months in, I dropped out. A couple of years later, I tried again but dropped out after five months. Finally, in 2011 when I was almost thirty-two years old and married with two kids, I realized I had procrastinated long enough. I needed to do something with my life and was tired of minimum wage jobs and the pressure of trying to provide for my family.

I enrolled in an accelerated program to get my associate's degree in business. The classes were fast paced with lots of quizzes and papers. Many times, I put off writing a paper until hours before it was due. That created conflict with the perfectionist in me, because I still wanted to get it "just right." This resulted in meltdowns—yelling at my family and bashing myself in "I can't do it" moments. While I always buckled down and turned everything in on time, I put my family through a lot of unnecessary stress.

However, when I went on to get my bachelor's in human services, I realized I had to get a grip on my procrastination, my perfectionism, and myself. I didn't like who I had become. I refused to let my family's happiness become the price I paid to get a college degree. I realized that it was more important to get the work done than to get it done perfectly. Family was important, too. So I got myself organized, scheduled regular times for study and writing, and reminded myself that I could do it by pacing myself rather than leaving the work until the last possible moment. I finished my bachelor's degree in eleven months with my GPA (3.89) just a little lower than my associate's (3.98).

Conquering procrastination is an important step toward maturity. It frees you from a lot of stress and worry and leads to a life that has a healthy balance of work and personal needs.

Amonie Keller has degrees in business administration and human services from Kaplan University. Currently, she is an administrative assistant for a charitable organization.

GOD'S LIFE LESSON

Whatever you do, work at it with
all your heart, as working for the Lord,
not for human masters, since you know
you will receive an inheritance
from the Lord as a reward.

COLOSSIANS 3:23–24

LIVING THE LESSON

- Write down your daily, weekly, and monthly tasks on a to-do list calendar so as to plan when you will complete each one.

- Simplify your life by clearing your schedule and home of the things you know bog you down so that you can focus on that which is important.

- Instead of overthinking each task set before you, just start the first one.

- Refuse to give in to distractions, such as online social media, television, and even music.

- Schedule your fun activities for a time after your task is completed. Use them as a reward.

Set goals to overcome complacency.

Susanna Morris Schwiesow

The biggest lesson I have learned in my life is that complacency is a killer. If you do not have a personal goal that you are trying to reach, it is very easy to be consumed with everyday, unimportant issues that will steal your joy. The best way to improve your life is by setting personal goals so that you are always working toward something. Why is this important? Because you were created to be a conqueror.

I wasn't always a conqueror. In fact, up until age thirty, I had branded myself a failure. I could practically see the word written on my forehead. I never took responsibility for my health and as a result became seriously overweight. I wanted to become a nurse and knew I would have to change my lifestyle and get healthy in order to do that.

I set a goal of losing eighty pounds in a year by exercising and changing my diet. I knew the only way I would be successful was if I made changes that I could sustain for the rest of my life. So I decided I would not count calories, but only eat whole, healthy foods. I also walked every day. These were changes I could sustain in my life long-term. I mapped out how much weight I wanted to lose every month, and then I rewarded myself if I made it. Every time I lost twenty pounds, I bought myself a new outfit. I am happy to say that I met my weight-loss goal for the first year.

Most successful people, set goals set measurable, achievable goals. Some examples are losing weight, gaining financial independence (such as living debt free), learning to play a musical instrument or speak a different language, or traveling out of the country. Whatever your goal, your soul is thirsty for a challenge to overcome. Goal setting will also teach you the great lesson of delayed gratification. While achieving your goal is a reward in itself, no part of the journey is wasted. The journey is where you learn what you are made of, how strong you truly are, and how you can trust God to get you through it. Life is not a dress rehearsal. Start working now toward the things you want in life and reap the benefits of them later. You will surprise yourself at how capable you really are.

Susanna Schwiesow has a nursing degree from Upper Iowa University and works in the field of nursing.

GOD'S LIFE LESSON

May he give you the desire of your heart
and make all your plans succeed.

PSALM 20:4

LIVING THE LESSON

- Decide on one personal goal—such as getting fit— and write it down.

- Once you set your goal, establish a realistic plan for meeting your goal. Set a deadline for yourself. If you're working on fitness, decide how, where, and when you will exercise.

- Tell someone else about your goal and plans and ask that person to check in with you periodically about your progress.

- Follow through with each step toward your goal.

- Choose pathway markers for rewards. When you meet your goal, celebrate it and then choose another goal.

Life's not a competition.

Niecea Freeman Wilson

How do I present myself to the world? How do I com-pare to others? These are questions I have asked myself since high school—on college applications and job resumes and even in my daily life as sculpted through social media. Where do *I* rank?

A few summers ago, I had the privilege of going to Thailand for a unique teaching opportunity. I was blessed with rich experiences and overwhelming support in my host country. However, because I found the need to let family and friends in the States be impressed with every-thing I was doing, I spent a silly amount of time updat-ing my social media profiles. Then, after uploading my photos to Facebook, I deleted all the moments from my camera, thinking that my profile was an adequate place to display and store my treasured memories. What I didn't realize was that social media sites compress your photos and downgrade the resolution of your content. So not only had I diminished my own experience in Thailand with my constant social media postings, I also had degraded the mementos I'd collected along the way.

The experience of losing my photos from this trip of a lifetime caused me to reflect on my need to impress others. Did I truly need to be better than my friends—more beautiful, more accomplished, more brilliant? I realized that my life up until then had been an internal competition of constantly trying to be better than others. My time abroad had been cheapened by a contest I had created for myself.

The truth is that, while I am significant, so are others. Life isn't a race; each of us is important for the tasks set before us. Since that time, I have shifted my attention to something much more valuable: living my life for the moment—unadulterated and unfiltered—so that I simply try to be the best person I can be, unmeasured against the achievements of others.

Niecea Freeman Wilson has an honors degree in integrated elementary education with an emphasis in English language acquisition from the University of Nevada, Reno. She is an educator and ELL intervention specialist.

GOD'S LIFE LESSON

We do not dare to classify or compare
ourselves with some who commend
themselves. When they measure themselves
by themselves and compare themselves
with themselves, they are not wise.

2 CORINTHIANS 10:12

LIVING THE LESSON

- When you find yourself comparing yourself to someone else, make a mental list of the good qualities that you have—and give thanks.

- Never slander someone else; that only reflects negatively on you anyway.

- Change those things about yourself that you can control—for example, eat healthier foods, get more exercise, or pursue a passion such as music.

- Be generous in celebrating others' accomplishments.

- Recognize that you will not always receive something you deserve, but you could also be rewarded for something you might not have deserved. Neither bitterness nor boasting in such cases is an attractive posture.

Contentment is more important than happiness.

Patrick Wilson

The pursuit of happiness. It is so deeply ingrained into American culture that our founding fathers declared it a fundamental right for every man. Yet, of the vast range of human emotions, none is so fleeting or elusive.

Growing up, I remember my dad being a hardworking man. He did everything he could to make sure my five brothers and I had everything we needed. This included taking a job in Saudi Arabia, where ten years later, he continues to work twelve-hour days as a safety engineer at a gas plant. His hobbies parallel his work: he is a man of endurance. He runs, bikes, and swims countless miles all over the world. He doesn't do these things because they are fun or because they give him pleasure; he does them because they are challenging and make him work hard and sweat. The man doesn't chase happiness; he confronts pain and has learned to be content.

Recently, I was struggling with the pursuit of happiness in my academic and personal life, and my dad gave me some advice that resonated with me. He stated simply, "You don't *need* to be happy." I remember laughing out loud. His words felt so contrary to everything I had heard before. I had always been told to chase happiness, to do the things that give me joy. Yet, I couldn't get his words out of my head.

The more I thought, the more I found an odd comfort in the idea that a person doesn't *need* to be happy. As I considered the most rewarding times of my life, I realized that my best stories aren't ones that are *happy*—I have learned more from my struggles than the times that were easy.

I finally feel free to take life as it comes—the highs and lows—and to appreciate the struggles, as they will lead not to happiness but to a deeper sense of contentment.

Patrick Wilson has a degree in integrated elementary education with an emphasis in early childhood education from the University of Nevada, Reno, and works as an elementary school teacher.

GOD'S LIFE LESSON

But seek first his kingdom
and his righteousness, and all these things
will be given to you as well.

MATTHEW 6:33

LIVING THE LESSON

- Pause for a moment and, even though life might be hard and stressful, find one thing you are grateful for right now.

- Keep yourself from saying something negative. Choose to be positive.

- Instead of waiting for happiness—that will probably never happen—pursue joy by doing those things that bring meaning to your life.

- Cultivate your friendships. Those who have deep relationships with people they know would support them through hard times are more satisfied with their lives.

- Consider becoming a big brother or big sister through the Big Brothers Big Sisters of America organization. When you are more focused on serving others, you get a broader perspective about your own personal struggles and help someone else in the process.

Integrity means keeping your word.

Jenny Roberti Gant

I've always been that person who has really good intentions. I *want* to stay in touch with my friends and family, to send nice just-because notes and attend get-togethers. I'd love to volunteer or surprise someone with a gift . . . so many things I'd like to do. Unfortunately, good intentions are not enough. Oftentimes I find myself saying I will do something or be somewhere—and I fully intend to do it—but then life gets in the way. Well, I *let* it get in the way.

I need to learn to be honest with myself about what I can and can't, will and won't actually do before I agree to something. If I think about it, I never mind when someone is upfront and honest, such as with saying, "Oh, that party sounds wonderful, but I can't make it that night. I'm sorry!" I do, however, mind when people say they *will* do something and then don't follow through. That just makes them flaky, and I might not believe them the next time. I love how the Bible phrases it: Let your *yes* be *yes* and your *no* be *no*. In other words, I need to be a person of honor who keeps her word. We all do.

At my grandpa's funeral, the pastor said something that really stuck with me: "Elmer was a man of his word and had true integrity. If everyone were like him, there would be no need for people to work at a bank. It could just be an unlocked building with a table of cash, and we could take only the amount that was ours." What an awesome testimony for him, but you and I can be like that, too.

It can take twenty years to build a reputation but just a few minutes to ruin it. Being a person of integrity means being intentional when you make a commitment—not just saying yes to maintain a comfort level for the moment, but because it is the right thing to do. Once you've committed to something, schedule the task and complete it as you said you would, to the best of your ability.

Jenny Gant has a degree in human development and family studies from the University of Nevada, Reno, with a master's in elementary education from Western Governors University. She taught fourth grade for a few years and now is a stay-at-home mom.

GOD'S LIFE LESSON

All you need to say is simply
"Yes" or "No"; anything beyond this
comes from the evil one.

MATTHEW 5:37

LIVING THE LESSON

- Avoid giving in to negative peer pressure that would cause you to make unwise decisions.

- To be a person of integrity, don't listen to gossip—and never spread it yourself.

- Research issues before making an on-the-spot decision about commitments.

- When you make a commitment, mark it on your calendar. If it involves something that you have to do in advance, make a reminder that precedes the deadline.

- Before making a long-term commitment, tell the individual involved that you would like to pray about accepting that responsibility—and then follow through with prayer.

People-pleasing is hazardous to your identity.

Tara Johnson

Pleasing people is a moving target that cannot be hit, although for years I tried. I answered every request with a yes and cheerfully performed whatever was asked of me—and no one knew how much resentment and anger I carried inside. I was desperate for approval, even if it meant losing myself in the process.

What we hide on the inside eventually becomes what we wear on the outside. In 2002 I was diagnosed with depression. Not every depression diagnosis is a result of people-pleasing, but I had beaten myself to a pulp trying to impress everyone around me. I thought approval equaled love, but I was wrong. The two are polar opposites. Approval is a stamp that says, "You meet my standards."

Love says, "You're a mess, but I'm crazy about you anyway." I had sought unconditional love in conditionally minded people, and that forced me to hide my true self with a plastic smile and a cracked heart.

Since then, God has transformed my walk with Him and has shown me what it means to walk in freedom. He designed each of us for a unique purpose before we ever drew a breath. How tragic to ignore His beautiful plan by pretending to be someone else. We are masterpieces, crafted by the very hands of God. There is no need to impress or to try to be "enough"—He's already declared how much we are loved when He stretched His arms wide upon the cross. Be yourself. Be vibrant. Be the masterpiece He created you to be. No one else can do it.

Tara Johnson, who has a degree in music from the University of Arkansas, is an author, speaker, and singer who homeschools her three children.

GOD'S LIFE LESSON

Am I now trying to win the approval
of human beings, or of God?
Or am I trying to please people?
If I were still trying to please people,
I would not be a servant of Christ.

GALATIANS 1:10

LIVING THE LESSON

- Realize that you have a choice in the matter—and saying no is one of those choices.

- Affirm others' ideas instead of just saying no. Say, "I love your idea—it has great value—but I can't take on that commitment right now."

- Understand that some people are good at manipulating others, so stand firm in what you believe you should or should not do.

- Explain your reasoning to the requester. Here's an example: "I've found lately that if I have evening commitments, I'm just not my best at work the next day."

- Pay attention to your own bad feelings. If you find yourself asking, "How and why did I get stuck with this?" learn from that situation so you don't repeat the behavior.

Learning from others
is part of education.

James Manion

An important lesson I learned in college was to stretch myself to appreciate new subjects.

Other people seemed to enjoy the oddest of topics, and I would wonder, "How on earth could anyone find this interesting?" These moments of personal bewilderment occurred regularly in college as I encountered an immensely diverse group of people. These individuals at first seemed quite alien, with minds that were completely enraptured by something that I hadn't even heard of before.

When I met people with radically different interests, I decided to learn more. I'd say, "Why exactly do you love what you love? Can you explain?" A friend once wisely told me that if I were intentional about learning about other people's interests, by the end of the conversation, I would find that the subject also piqued my attention. For example, maybe you like engineering, but others are fascinated with English or history. Ask them why that subject interests them. Maybe they are studying something that sounds bizarre, like Ciceronian Latin or Euclidian geometry. That's even better! Most of the time, their answers will be surprisingly understandable and deeply human. No doubt asking for their explanation will also bring a smile to their face.

Let the love and excitement of others permeate into your life. Surround yourself with people who are in love with different things from you and let their hearts teach you to appreciate that which was previously obscure. Finally, take a moment to ask yourself, "Why exactly do I love what I love?" You might be pleasantly surprised that, once you have put the answer into words, your own explanation can inspire you again and serve as a reminder to carry on the journey of learning.

James Manion graduated from Hillsdale College with a degree in political economics and religion. He is working as a middle school teacher.

GOD'S LIFE LESSON

———————

Let the wise listen
and add to their learning,
and let the discerning get guidance.

PROVERBS 1:5

LIVING THE LESSON

- Take interest in others' unique interests by asking relevant questions. Most people appreciate sincere questions.

- To continue the conversation, do some online research yourself about the topic. This will demonstrate your respect for the person and interest in the idea.

- Don't be afraid to collaborate with others on a project. Bring your talents and knowledge to the table and then look for others' expertise. Work together, maximizing each other's abilities.

- Listen to podcasts on various subjects to make yourself more well rounded.

- Find a mentor who could teach you about a subject you are not familiar with. Meet regularly over lunch or coffee.

Identity is
a soul-searching process.

Natalie Davis

I started my senior year in college incredibly ready and excited to graduate into the next chapter of my life. Then I increasingly became nervous and felt lost as I was nearing the end of my final semester. I began wondering if I would get the job I wanted and if I would have an opportunity to make a difference in the world through it. I worried about what goals I should set. I was unsure how a job would impact my identity—how it would define me and perhaps even change me.

I started researching, both online and face-to-face with people who had "been there, done that." I remember coming across a website that laid out everything I was feeling—and why I shouldn't feel so uncertain. It was a reminder that, while what we do in our careers does impact our future, the job itself—what we do on a daily basis to earn a living—does not define who we are nor how we make a lasting impression with our lives.

Because my identity is in Jesus Christ, my purpose is found through my relationship with Him. Therefore, my life is meaningful because of Him. I am but a vessel, called to use my gifts to serve Him. Sharing my faith and making a difference in others' lives need not only be done by working in a nonprofit in another country; I can live out my faith in any workplace.

It may sound silly to some, but the fear of not making a difference through my career and not finding a job where I could do so bothered me for months. I am grateful for friends and family who encouraged me and for the writer of the words I needed to see. They truly changed my perspective—from thinking my career defined my identity and life's purpose to surrendering my identity to Jesus Christ. Christ's presence in my life provides purpose and direction. As I serve Him everywhere, my workplace becomes only a part of that focus. This understanding has brought peace and joy into my life as I live out my true identity.

Natalie Davis has a degree in integrative studies with a concentration in organizational administration from George Mason University. She currently coordinates a university department that supports its international students.

GOD'S LIFE LESSON

We are God's workmanship,
created in Christ Jesus to do good works,
which God prepared in advance for us to do.

EPHESIANS 2:10

LIVING THE LESSON

- Pursue your interests, strengths, passions, and curiosity as you job seek so that your work is a natural fit that doesn't grow tedious and uninteresting.

- Understand what your weaknesses are, and make personal growth goals in those areas.

- Learn more about your personality—such as whether you're an introvert or extrovert, an organizer or follower, a feeler or a thinker.

- Think about your internal clock—whether you are a morning person or a night person—so that you can maximize your energy during the day for creativity and problem solving.

- Read a little bit of the Bible daily, so that it speaks truth into your heart about who you are and what purpose God has for you to fulfill here on earth.

Befriend strangers and newcomers.

Adam Loveridge

Some of the people who have brought the most meaning to my life are those whom I wouldn't have met, let alone become friends with, if I hadn't intentionally sought them out to learn from them. I grew up in a small, rural town and was taught to be afraid of the city. I remember my grandfather locking the car doors as we drove through San Francisco, so no one could get us when we stopped at a red light. Further, because I am an introvert, I find it difficult to initiate conversation with new people, especially those from different cultures. *What if I say the wrong thing? What if I offend them?* But learning to take those risks has greatly enriched my life.

My third year at college, I was asked to go on a six-week

summer project to work at a Boys and Girls Club in the inner city of Los Angeles. I nervously said yes. There I met amazing kids and became friends with adults who spoke languages and ate foods that were strange to me. The kids from the Boys and Girls Club and my new adult friends showed me that we had much more in common than I would have thought if I had just passed them on the street. While their perspectives were much different than mine, they were just as important and valuable. I realized during that summer project that there was beauty in the world that I was missing by staying in the comfort of a community that looked just like me.

That summer project gave me the boldness to continue befriending people who are different than I am. Learning how to navigate cultural differences around me is complex. I'm a white man with a lot of privilege and have come to realize that, unless I choose to intentionally befriend and learn from others who are different than I am, not only am I missing out, but I'm also often unwittingly contributing to the oppression that keeps us divided. I need the stranger and the newcomer because they see things that I don't.

Ultimately, my experience of the divine is expanded when I welcome, learn from, and befriend those who are different from me. We can either stay in our bubble and let fear and judgment isolate us or embrace the beauty in the diversity around us.

Adam Loveridge has a degree in architecture from Cal Poly, San Luis Obispo, and just finished a program in the art of spiritual direction from San Francisco Theological Seminary. He is regional staff coordinator for a college Christian organization.

GOD'S LIFE LESSON

After this I looked, and there before me was a great multitude that no one could count, from every nation, tribe, people and language, standing before the throne and before the Lamb. They were wearing white robes and were holding palm branches in their hands.

REVELATION 7:9

LIVING THE LESSON

- When you are part of a community or small group, look for the people who are new and introduce yourself. Then, introduce them to other folks you know.

- When talking with a person from a different culture, ask about the traditions his or her family celebrates.

- Challenge yourself to learn a new language and then use it with people who use it as their first language.

- Attend a cultural festival in your area. For example, one city has these among many others: Latin Food and Music Festival, Pacific Rim Street Fest, and Black Book Fair.

- Try new restaurants with a foreign flair, and ask other customers in the restaurant for their recommendations.

The easiest path may not be the best one.

Brian May

One avenue of life may seem easier than another, but that does not mean it is the best one to take. In college, I had to make many tough decisions on my own for the first time—all the way from simple meal planning and grocery shopping to giving up my dream of becoming a professional baseball player to concentrate on school and ultimately a career.

The decision that stands out the most to me, however, was whether I should take a nonmajor course in my senior year, when I still wasn't clear on what I wanted to do with my life. That summer, a friend told me about a challenging but very interesting class she'd taken: farm and ranch appraisal. I was interested, but the course was not an acceptable class for the college of business. I scheduled an appointment with the dean to see if he would sign off on the class. I walked into his office, confident with the case I had put together . . . and three minutes later walked out with his answer. No.

I wanted to register a complaint, to argue why the course should have been allowed toward my major requirements. I didn't want to take an extra class in my senior year—one that would be challenging with four additional credits above my full-time load. I momentarily considered dropping the extra course. However, my gut said I needed to take that extra class, regardless of the difficulties. So I did . . . and it was the best decision I made in college.

Yes, the class was tough, but I enjoyed its analytical, problem-solving, and comparison aspects and how they directly applied to real-world situations. In fact, that extra course, the only one that did not count toward my major, ultimately led me to my career. If I had decided to make my life easier and not take the course, I wouldn't have found the career I am enjoying today.

Brian May has a degree in business finance from California State University, Chico, and works as a risk adjustment supervisor for a healthcare organization.

GOD'S LIFE LESSON

Consider it pure joy, my brothers
and sisters, whenever you face trials
of many kinds, because you know
that the testing of your faith
produces perseverance.

JAMES 1:2–3

LIVING THE LESSON

- When you have a tough decision to make, create a pros and cons list to aid in the process.

- Also consider cause-and-effect reasoning. Ask yourself what could result if you do the thing you're considering, and what could happen if you don't.

- If you're confused, pretend you are advising a friend. What counsel would you give him or her?

- Understand how your personal bias (or even laziness) colors your decision-making process. No one really wants to make life difficult for himself or herself, but the outcome of that hard work could be satisfying.

- Consider that days pass, and sometimes you'll experience seasons that are tougher than others—for example, an extra heavy load at the workplace. Do your best, so you are proud of yourself and your work.

Education is
a lifelong process.

Gino Folchi

When my undergraduate work was done, I thought, *Whew, I'm glad those seventeen years are behind me!* What I didn't yet understand was that, for those who want to keep growing personally and professionally, education is a lifelong process. I finally figured that out after a doctor's visit sometime in my late twenties.

"I have bad news for you," the doctor said. "You are done growing vertically, and it's all horizontal from here on out." After half my life working, playing, and sometimes living outside, the party was over. A strange word was uttered. *Metabolism,* he called it. It had the same ring as *APR* in a car commercial. I sort of had an idea what it meant but wasn't ready to give a textbook definition.

I tell this to every student intern on his or her first day: "If you have a question, try solving it on your own first. You have the world at your fingertips. It's called the Internet." Taking my own advice, I read up on how the body changes when you approach thirty. There were no exams or notes, just a voluntary pursuit of knowledge to better myself and hopefully stave off inevitable weight gain—and I learned a lot. *Metabolism* is no longer a foreign word, but exercising the needed muscles will require more than reading a book.

The brain is also a muscle that requires exercise, however, and it will suffer without it. Information has never been as free and available as it is today. Your smartphone has more computing power than NASA had in 1969. Keep exercising that muscle in your head, if for no other reason than to find new interests.

Gino Folchi is a graduate of George Mason University, with a degree in political science. He works as a public relations professional and is attending law school.

GOD'S LIFE LESSON

The heart of the discerning
acquires knowledge,
for the ears of the wise seek it out.

PROVERBS 18:15

LIVING THE LESSON

- Don't rely solely on social media for news: read several different news sources daily to keep informed.

- Read books of interest outside your comfort zone.

- Look up words you don't know to keep building your personal vocabulary.

- If you don't understand something, ask pertinent questions.

- Take lessons in a skill completely new for you—such as cooking, guitar playing, or painting—and then create something. Exercising creativity develops problem-solving skills, because when you solve a problem, you are creating a solution.

You can be a peacemaker.

Kayla Gressel

World travel gripped my imagination at a young age. Through both good fortune and hard work, I have had the pleasure of experiencing many different countries and cultures over the course of ten years through study abroad and other programs. However, it was only recently that I discovered my passion to travel for its joy alone was waning, because I was collecting experiences to only enrich myself. I was taking wonderful experiences from each place I visited, but all I was doing, ultimately, was *taking*.

One day on a train ride through Vietnam I thought, *This beautiful place has given me so much—but what will I give this country in return?* A revelation came to me: for as much good I receive from the world, I should give. To every place I go, I should take a little bit of peace. I discovered endless opportunities to volunteer and get involved with communities in Vietnam; all it took was the time and effort to seek them out.

A friend in India gave me the wonderful idea to donate five dollars from every paycheck to a charity or nonprofit. Rather than ignore or be overwhelmed by social or economic issues anywhere on the planet, we can all take small actions to foster positive change, whether for our hometown, our nation, or our fellow humans living in different parts of the world. We can contribute to community wherever we find ourselves in the world. For as much as we take, we can give—extending a little bit of peace to every place we go.

Kayla Gressel, who has a degree in peace and conflict studies from Colgate University, is a graduate student in security studies at Georgetown University, currently studying language and culture in Vietnam.

GOD'S LIFE LESSON

Let us therefore make every effort
to do what leads to peace
and to mutual edification.

ROMANS 14:19

LIVING THE LESSON

- To be a peacemaker, start by recognizing your part in the equation. If you tend to be argumentative or critical, listen more. Notice what others are doing right and affirm them.

- When you offend someone, admit your wrong-doing and ask forgiveness.

- Seek opportunities to be a peacemaker. Be a mediator between arguing parties. Stick up for those who are bullied.

- Make a difference in your community. For example, you could coordinate an effort to collect stuffed animals or set up a library at a children's hospital.

- Help your church or other local nonprofit organization raise funds for its causes.

Doing more than
the minimum is rewarding.

Jessica Anglin

Often, doing the bare minimum is the easiest route to take through life. For some people, that's all they do. There have been times when my life was unfulfilled and even boring. Upon reflection, those were the times I was doing the bare minimum as I moved through life. But when I take initiative and do more than the minimum, I find more happiness and fulfillment.

For example, during my preprofessional internship, I worked under an outreach coordinator. Many of the duties I needed to fulfill would have easily qualified my internship for credit. I could have just done those basic duties and been in and out in three months, but I wanted more out of my internship than simple credit, so I chose to do extra, unpaid hours. I had no idea where my extra work would lead me except for perhaps a stronger recommendation, but I made myself professionally available to not only my supervisor but other employees as well. By the end of my first month of internship, I was offered a paid position in a field of work that hadn't ever crossed my mind in all my studies as a student—and it's a job I love.

When I started college, I was just going for a degree. By the time I finished college, I had a full-time job because I had learned that putting forth some initiative could not only help me but also lead to fulfillment in ways I hadn't previously considered.

———————

Jessica Anglin has degrees in human development and family studies from Colorado State University. After serving in the US Navy, she worked professionally as a nanny and is now an infant development specialist and parenting consultant.

GOD'S LIFE LESSON

May the favor of the Lord our God
rest on us; establish the work
of our hands for us—yes, establish
the work of our hands.

PSALM 90:17

LIVING THE LESSON

- When your company adopts a new policy, be the first employee to put that new procedure into place.

- Be the person who picks up the remnants of paper in the copy room at work.

- Look for ways to simplify a process on your job or to save money—then volunteer to put that new process into place.

- If you know that a coworker likes a certain coffee drink, pick one up on your way to work.

- If a project requires someone from the staff to work extra hours, be that person who volunteers.

- Take along a trash bag as you head out for your daily run or walk and pick up trash.

Laughter is healthy.

Andrea McCurtis Keeshan

Life can often be hectic and filled with not-so-fun demands. At times, it almost seems easier to add more to the to-do list than to scratch something from it. Whether it's final exams, an onslaught of papers and projects due, a relationship situation, or a deadline at work, it's easy to grit your teeth, buckle up, and get on the hamster-wheel-of-life just to maintain. Some may call this killer focus; others, a death sentence. I call it forgetting to laugh.

I was burning some serious calories on the wheel while finishing my bachelor's degree. I was enrolled in twenty-one units, working twenty-plus hours at a coffee shop, copyediting once a week, teaching twice a week, and keeping a very full extracurricular calendar. Consequently, I was sick all the time and not really enjoying anything I had my hands in. I had become so focused on what needed to be done and how I was going to manage it all that taking care of myself had become a side note. Obviously, something needed to change. I realized that no matter what I did, unless I took the time to refuel my heart, mind, and body, I wouldn't have anything left to give anywhere else.

That's when I learned self-care is not selfish but imperative. Self-care looks different for each person. One simple and effective way I take care of myself is by laughing every day. There's a ton of research on the health benefits of laughter. Personally, I think it's way better than running on a treadmill. Laughter can be effective in big and small doses—there is no quantity to the prescription. Sometimes I laugh from reading a humorous article or watching a favorite sitcom or movie. Sometimes a good friend and I text jokes, or I look through old videos on my phone of fun moments with family and friends.

Regardless of the medium, I always feel better after engaging in some laughter. Laughter won't solve exhaustion or overscheduling, but it can give you the boost you need to keep going for the demands of the moment . . . or even a season.

Andrea Keeshan has a degree in communication studies with an emphasis on digital video from California State University, Sacramento. Currently, she is in the graduate counselor education program at Sacramento State to become a school counselor.

GOD'S LIFE LESSON

A cheerful heart is good medicine,
but a crushed spirit dries up the bones.

PROVERBS 17:22

LIVING THE LESSON

- Learn to laugh at yourself. Self-deprecating humor makes people seem more real and approachable. Turn a mistake into something funny to share with a friend.

- Choose a romantic comedy when you go to the movies; read the daily comics in the morning; or read books that have a light approach, such as Douglas Adams's *The Hitchhiker's Guide to the Galaxy*, a science-fiction comedy.

- Adjust your environment to prompt your smiles by adding fun objects. One church gave out stress balls with a silly face on them that, when squeezed, the eyes pop out. Putting something funny like that on your work desk could coerce out a laugh.

- Be lighthearted, but don't worry about being funny. Not all people are good at telling jokes or making witty puns. You can, however, focus on the positive during your day and approach others with a smile.

- Look for humor around you. Even sharing a cat video with a coworker during a lunch break can ease tension on the job.

Siblings can be your best friends.

Beth Cheek Whitacre

At any given time in life, I could have murdered each one of my siblings without remorse. My older sister was the worst. She was the mom of the other siblings, the tattletale, and enemy number one. She was relentless in her need to know everything that was going on with all of us, making sure we were doing what she thought was best. My younger siblings were just in the way. I had to be nice to them, even if they weren't nice to me. I learned all about the *s* word—*sharing* . . . by far one of the worst words in the English language.

At the age of eighteen, I moved to the southernmost city on the planet for a year. Halfway across the globe in Argentina, I finally experienced freedom from my controlling and annoying siblings. I also gained perspective on what it means to be a part of a family. I began to understand that my two sisters and brother simply loved me and wanted the best for me. No matter where I've been since then—away at college or on travels around the world, I have never once questioned my family's love or loyalty.

I've also understood that their characteristics that drove me to tears then are now the driving force that keeps our relationships strong and supportive. They love me unconditionally, as I do them. My personal experience growing up with these crazy people has proven time and again that, no matter where we go or what we do, we are there for each other. Even on those days we don't feel like showing up for each other or don't particularly like each other, we are still family and love each other deeply.

I'm glad I've learned to appreciate my family. Even though siblings can drive you crazy, they truly are one of life's best gifts.

Beth Whitacre has a degree from Texas Christian University in social work. Formerly an international adoption specialist, she is now a full-time mom to her and her husband's adopted son from Colombia.

GOD'S LIFE LESSON

Be kind and compassionate
to one another, forgiving each other,
just as in Christ God forgave you.

EPHESIANS 4:32

LIVING THE LESSON

- Keep the past in the past. Everyone squabbles with brothers and sisters growing up. Forgive them their mistakes—as you hope they will forgive yours.

- Stop perpetuating family gossip; it only divides family members.

- Remember each sibling's birthday; send a card and call.

- Take a trip with just your sibling(s) to create your own special memories.

- Work with your siblings to organize an annual family reunion—even if it's just a daylong experience, it will create important memories for you all.

Perfection is overrated.

Jessica West–DeJarnatt

When I was in elementary school, my dad told me he thought I needed to fail something, just to know that it wouldn't be the end of my world. I quickly learned that I would constantly struggle with my need for perfection.

In high school I was preparing for an oral defense of a paper I'd written. In that same deadline week, a close family friend died from ovarian cancer. That loss helped me put my stress-filled preparations for the presentation into perspective.

While I daily confront my struggle with perfectionism, my demanding work with students with disabilities sometimes means my work is imperfect. The nature of my job often requires me to reprioritize my to-do list at a moment's notice as I model for my students and my staff an imperfect yet confident and flexible professional. Because I know that time is a factor in all things and that limitations are real, I'm able to choose every day what's important. This often means that being intentional and genuine takes priority over presenting a perfect product. And when I forget and start going back to that place of desiring perfection, I am lucky enough to have people in my life who remind me of just what's important, so I can let go of that obsession.

Jessica West-DeJarnatt has a degree in psychology from Western Washington University and a master's in special education with an emphasis in applied behavior analysis from the University of Washington. She currently works as a behavior analyst with middle school students who have autism and other related disabilities.

GOD'S LIFE LESSON

As for God, his way is perfect:
the LORD's word is flawless;
he shields all who take refuge in him.

PSALM 18:30

LIVING THE LESSON

- Know the difference between healthy and obsessive perfectionism. It is important to complete a job to the best of your ability, given time constraints. However, losing sleep and becoming an emotional wreck is not healthy.

- Be consistent about your health: eat well, exercise, and get enough sleep.

- Abandon the mindset that a task is all or nothing. Complete the job to the best of your ability in the time you have.

- Break down large tasks into smaller components with a time schedule for completion of each of those smaller bites.

- When you catch yourself berating yourself for your mistakes, make a mental list of what you have done well recently. The good will undoubtedly outweigh the mistakes.

Giving generously is rewarding.

Chelsea Adams Valdés

I clearly remember the day that changed the purpose of my life. I had recently moved to Chile to teach English in a school in a very poor neighborhood. My heart went out to a twelve-year-old student one day when she told me her father had been killed the night before. When my husband and I went to her home to lead the funeral service, I was shocked. Her ceiling was hanging down from water damage to about the height of my waist. While I had known the girl was poor, seeing the poverty was another story. As we walked out of her house that day, my husband and I started talking about how we could help, even though we didn't have enough to pay our own rent at the time. How could we possibly fix up their living conditions? A couple months later, we started a fund-raising campaign to fix up some of our students' houses, more specifically, their rooms, so they could have a place to study and break the vicious cycle of poverty. Several national television stations aired our story, which helped us get materials we needed.

Then one day, one of our volunteers asked us to go with her to meet with a family. There I saw poverty in its most raw form. About forty houses built of trash were stuck on top of a very steep hill. The smell was something I would never forget: trash, mud, and spoiled food blended into a scent that I call "infection"—the odor of disease. For several hours, we talked to this family, and then I watched as a one-year-old boy went down to a mountain of trash, pulled out a half-eaten sopapilla, and ate it. How could this be real? How had I never gone more than a day without eating, while this child was eating from the garbage? My husband and I left crying that night, knowing life would never be the same again. We would give of our time, love, and resources to serve these people.

Of course, not everyone can move to South America and fight poverty, but people can make a difference in the world by caring enough to share what they have and seek to truly help others who are not as fortunate as they are.

Chelsea Valdés has a degree in recreation management from Sierra College. She serves as director of El Mejor Cambio de Tu Vida, the nonprofit organization that she and her husband, Jairo, founded. She also works as an English teacher.

GOD'S LIFE LESSON

Whoever is kind to the poor lends
to the LORD, and he will reward them
for what they have done.

PROVERBS 19:17

LIVING THE LESSON

- Support an overseas child through an organization such as World Vision or Compassion International.

- Keep small lunch bags of food in your car to give to the homeless.

- If a family member or friend has surgery or an extended illness, organize meals for that person through an online network such as Take Them a Meal or Meal Train.

- Give first out of your paycheck to a charity or your church before you pay your monthly bills—you won't notice it.

- If you'd like to participate in a short-term crowd-funding campaign through a platform such as Go Fund Me, give up something just for one month (such as eating fast food), and donate the money to that cause.

Interruptions can be opportunities.

Rebekah McHenry Perez

Life is all about interruptions, and we have to learn to roll with them. Whether it's a child who needs our attention, a friend who stops by to talk, or something far more life-changing, how we handle the experience will define our character.

I have six young children. Six. People think my husband and I are insane. Every day feels like one long, ongoing interruption. I remember one day when my feisty youngest daughter quietly busied herself while the other kids and I focused on schoolwork. In less than fifteen minutes, she had shoved an entire roll of toilet paper down the bathroom sink, emptied tubes of pink and blue toothpaste all over the boys' room carpet, and spread about two hundred children's books around the laundry room. I spent hours that day unclogging my sink and scrubbing carpet, and I didn't have a good attitude about any of it. I was so angry with my daughter for "ruining my day." Ironically, she later told me that she was trying to make the boys' room look pretty with all the different colors.

Interruptions are an ever-present reminder that I am not in charge of my life. God orders my steps. Every time I'm interrupted, I have the responsibility to answer in a way that glorifies Him, even in stressful circumstances. While I'm still working on this process, I am now aware that often the interruption is actually the opportunity—or even the most beautiful experience—of my day.

Rebekah Perez holds bachelor's and master's degrees in English education, both from Biola University. She formerly worked as an English educator and currently is homeschooling her children and teaching elective classes part-time.

GOD'S LIFE LESSON

There is a time for everything,
and a season for every activity
under the heavens.

ECCLESIASTES 3:1

LIVING THE LESSON

- Admit that interruptions may not come from outside sources as much as your own tendencies to check email and your phone.

- Create a prioritized to-do list for each day, so that as interruptions occur, you can focus more quickly on that which needs to be done.

- Plan for interruptions by not procrastinating on projects, so that you can demonstrate kindness to the person who might pull you from your work.

- When life sends a major interruption, make a list of possible blessings that could occur because of this life change.

- Recognize that creative solutions often come as a result of interruptions.

Beauty is all around us.

Crystal Dryden Emsoff

I grew up in the Sierra Valley, perched on the northeastern edge of the Sierra Nevada mountain range in northern California. Cited as the largest alpine valley in the United States, it has no shortage of breathtaking scenery—from emerald hay fields to bird-filled wetlands to pine-studded mountains circling the valley with their protective embrace. As a teenager, I would walk my dogs to the meadow behind our home, lie in the grass, and watch the clouds drift overhead. As I listened to the birds chirping in the nearby willows, I would talk to God. This was where I found my peace from the typical teenager turmoil. This was where I saw God in His creation and where I felt the closest to Him.

When I headed off to college in Texas, I found myself surrounded by concrete, asphalt, and people. At first, I couldn't find God there. One night, I was sitting in a worship service, feeling so downhearted that it was hard even to sing. And then God gently whispered in my ear, "*This is My creation.*" I was stunned. He was right! I had been so focused on seeing God's natural world creation, I had missed His most magnificent creation right in front of me: His people.

I'd like to say I didn't lose sight of that simple lesson over the next four years, but there were still times I longed for peaceful, wide open places to get alone with God. In those times, I was able to remind myself, however, of what He taught me that night and be comforted. After college I returned to my beloved Sierra Valley with my new husband, where we started our family.

Even though I'm back in the place I so dearly love, life continues to throw challenges our way, as it does for everyone. Nonetheless, I can look around me and see the blessings He has for me, whether in the faces of my children or the vastness of the star-filled night sky. In my surroundings, I can always find peace and joy.

Crystal Emsoff has a bachelor's degree in animal science from Abilene Christian University and now runs her own sheep ranch.

GOD'S LIFE LESSON

The heavens declare the glory of God;
the skies proclaim the work of his hands.

PSALM 19:1

LIVING THE LESSON

- Take a five-minute pause in your day to quiet yourself, breathe, and appreciate the beauty of nature around you.

- Go on a hike or camp in a nearby park.

- Invest in a pair of binoculars so you can better observe wildlife in nature areas.

- Drive to a rural area in the evening to stargaze.

- As you travel to a new place, take some pictures of the scenery to remind yourself of the landscape.

- Have some of those photo memories printed in enlargements to frame for inexpensive artwork.

- Notice other senses in natural surroundings—smell, touch, sound, and even the taste of salty air near the ocean.

Courage can be summoned.

Fallon Turner Stover

Courage is a combination of grit, grace, and heart. You won't know how much you have until you have to overcome overwhelming odds. For every person, there is a time in his or her life when something is daunting, where bravery is tested and tried. I once thought I had courage, at least in a rudimentary sense—when it came to competing in events, public speaking, and other intimidating things— but true courage requires much more, as I would learn.

Shortly before high school graduation, I was in a life-altering car accident. I found myself fighting for my life. My whole world changed in an instant. I lost my mother in that accident, and I had significant injuries—so much so that I was unable to attend my own commencement ceremony. Nevertheless, I reached deep down, found courage, and never looked back. I never questioned myself, because the alternatives were unacceptable. I took hold of grit, grace, and heart to heal physically, emotionally, and spiritually. Yes, my life had changed dramatically, but I didn't let it stop me from having the courage to chase my dreams. I worked through rehabilitation and went off to college that next fall.

I learned how to use courage, have faith in myself, and fight for what I really wanted. You have to find that small piece of something that keeps you moving forward. You must summon the strength to tune out the naysayers, the grace to move past your failures or mistakes, and the grit or determination to make your dreams come true. No matter the challenge, you can be brave and succeed. One day you will look back to that first trial to understand how far you have come.

––––––––––––

Fallon Turner Stover graduated from California Polytechnic State University, San Luis Obispo, majoring in animal science, with a minor in range management. She now is chasing her dreams as a sixth generation cattle rancher.

GOD'S LIFE LESSON

Be on your guard;
stand firm in the faith;
be courageous; be strong.

1 CORINTHIANS 16:13

LIVING THE LESSON

- Face your fears by scripting or mentally rehearsing a response to them.

- Acknowledge that you may have exaggerated the object of your fears.

- Decide that you are bigger than your fears and equipped to deal with them.

- If your fear relates to something like having your blood drawn, remember that millions of people have done that before you.

- Summon courage bit by bit by breaking your vision down into small steps, then tackle them one at a time to reach your goal.

Acknowledgments

I am so thankful for all the young contributors to this project, most of whom were my own students at Loyalton High School their junior and senior years. I am proud of them and their peers. While I may have taught them a little something, they have enriched my life and given me reason to celebrate their successes and purpose-filled lives. Go Grizzlies!

I am also appreciative of my loving husband, children, and family, who all grace me with their understanding and support as I write about those ideas closest to my heart.

This book would not have happened without the wise counsel and friendship of my agent, Janet Grant, the vision of my editor, Pamela Clements, and the really cool folks at Worthy Publishing. Thank you for understanding that young voices need to be heard.

Lastly, I pray that this project is indeed worthy of the One who called me to write many years ago and whom I still serve.

About the Editor

For many years, Janet Holm McHenry taught high school English and served as academic advisor in her small town. She still interacts with students through her Senior Year 101 blog and as the official scorekeeper for her school's home basketball games. Janet also volunteers as a board of directors officer for The Sierra Schools Foundation, a nonprofit that raises and provides grant funds for children's programs in her rural school district. She is a national speaker and the author of twenty-two books, including the best-selling *PrayerWalk*. Janet and her husband, Craig, live in Northern California's Sierra Valley, where they raised their four children—all of whom have finished college, are now married, and are gainfully employed in jobs they love. Janet appreciates hearing from readers and may be contacted through her Looking Up! business at www.janetmchenry.com. She would love to speak to your organization.

IF YOU ENJOYED THIS BOOK, WILL YOU CONSIDER SHARING THE MESSAGE WITH OTHERS?

Mention the book in a blog post or through Facebook, Twitter, or upload a picture through Instagram.

Recommend this book to those in your small group, book club, workplace, and classes.

Head over to facebook.com/worthypublishing, "LIKE" the page, and post a comment as to what you enjoyed the most.

Tweet "I recommend reading #50LifeLessons by @ Janet McHenery // @WorthyPub"

Pick up a copy for someone you know who would be challenged and encouraged by this message.

Write a book review online.

WORTHY®
PUBLISHING

Visit us at worthypublishing.com

twitter.com/worthypub

youtube.com/worthypublishing

facebook.com/worthypublishing

instagram.com/worthypub